M000211560

Harder Than I Thought,
Easier Than I Feared

Harder Than I Thought, Easier Than I Feared

SPORTS, ANXIETY, AND THE POWER OF MEDITATION

BILLY HANSEN

Harder Than I Thought, Easier Than I Feared
Copyright © 2021 Billy Hansen
All rights reserved.

ISBN Paperback: 978-1-7368728-0-2
ISBN Audiobook: 978-1-7368728-1-9
ISBN Ebook: 978-1-7368728-2-6

Cover art by Studio&.nl
Layout by Sue Balcer

Billyhansen.net

This book contains information about my own issues in mental health, and what helped me overcome them. What I write is not intended as a substitute for the medical advice of physicians or mental health professionals. The reader should consult a physician in matters relating to his/her mental health and particularly with respect to any symptoms that may require diagnosis or medical attention.

For Oma, Opa, Mom and Dad

CONTENTS

INTRODUCTION..1

1 GHOSTY ON FIRST 7

2 VARSITY 11

3 RECRUITED 17

4 FALLING OUT OF BOUNDS...............................21

5 LETTER OF INTENT 31

6 IMPOSTER 39

7 THE SPIRAL...47

8 SPORTS AND IDENTITY 59

9 MENTAL TRAINING...65

10 ADDING WOOD TO THE FIRE 73

11 BABY STEPS..83

12 CATCHING UP TO THE CAR...............................91

13 THE INNER GAME...99

14 NEW CULTURE..113

15 LOVE AND LUCK 121

16 BETTER HABITS 125

17 MENTAL BALANCE 135

18 THE BLUE TEAM 141

19 LETTING IT FLY...145

20 FLOW 151

21 CONNECTION 165

22 MENTAL HEALTH IN SPORTS 171

23 THE MEDICINE OF PRACTICE.........................187

24 INSIGHTS...197

25 LIFE AFTER SPORTS...217

ACKNOWLEDGMENTS...225

ABOUT THE AUTHOR...229

INTRODUCTION

When I touched my phone's home button the screen flashed 4:12 a.m. Pressure rose in my chest. I wanted to roll over and go back to sleep, but I had to be at the gym by 5:00 at the latest to allow time to have my ankles taped and then warm up for a 5:45 practice. So I lay there flat on my back for eighteen precious minutes.

The alarm finally buzzed, and I stumbled out of bed, inserted my contacts, and dressed in the warmest dirty clothes I could find from the pile on my floor. Upstairs I found my roommate lifelessly stirring a Chobani yogurt. We communicated our shared misery by doing nothing to acknowledge one another. As we left the house I grabbed a protein bar.

Dressed much like Eskimos, we speed-walked across the campus toward the gym. I thought about what I wished was different, longing for comfort and ease, like lazy Sunday mornings with Mom's egg burritos and Seinfeld reruns—but then, back in reality, I counted the months left in basketball season. I envied teammates who were lucky enough to be injured and could miss practice. Why couldn't I catch some luck and sprain an ankle? My mood grew darker when I remembered that I was unprepared for a chemistry test at 10. Instead of napping after practice, I'd have to cram for an exam.

I felt sure I'd have another lousy practice. What would I do if I missed another layup in the weave drill, or air-balled a shot in our scrimmage? Entering the gym, I wondered if Coach would take my scholarship away during the offseason. Then I was distracted by, "Mornin', Bill!" along with a friendly smile from my friend and teammate Jarrett. Even though I'd seen his morning smiles for months, the cheerfulness surprised me.

"What's up, man?" was the best reply I could think of.

With my feet extended past the end of a bench, our athletic trainer taped my ankles with the same repetitious monotony that I experience when I brush my teeth. He seemed no happier than I was to be at the gym at 5 in the morning, but the firm security of taped ankles was a subtle pleasure in the midst of my anxiety.

Based on how we dressed down in silence, an outside observer would have found it easy to estimate our team's record. Out on the court some teammates were shooting around. Hands feeling stiff and awkward, I grabbed a ball off the rack and dribbled toward the hoop. After looking up to the balcony at Coach's office to make sure he wasn't watching, I took a breath and held it. A few feet from the basket, I tossed up a shot that ricocheted off the rim and bounced away. At least I'd hit the rim.

I had time for a few mid-range shots before Coach arrived. The sight of him induced a mild state of panic, and my goal became the usual—surviving practice without exposing myself as the inferior player I'd somehow become. Day after day, this had been my mindset through my sophomore season.

Two years earlier things had been very different. In high school I'd led the state in scoring and broken multiple records, and made 10 three-pointers in a single game. Now I couldn't imagine ever playing that well again. The best I could hope to do was hide my feelings from my coach, my friends, and my family, and somehow manage to survive my college basketball career.

* * *

As a sophomore at Regis I found myself hopelessly miserable; and as a senior I enjoyed the most satisfying season of my life. My path from depression and anxiety to joy and peak performance was unconventional. I saw a therapist, who taught me the practice of meditation, and encouraged me to face my problems instead of shrinking from them. I formed a new, durable sense of identity. I modified my habits with drugs, partying, and my phone. I read great, old books. And I developed an entirely new attitude toward my sport and my life.

Since graduating, I've been committed to meditation, studying the practice and working with other young athletes, helping them develop their own practices and face the same problems I faced in sports and life. In this book I have three primary objectives:

1. I want athletes to understand that their confidence issues, insecurities, self-doubt, feelings of imposter syndrome, and tendency to wish days, weeks, and entire seasons away are commonplace in athletics. I explore new, effective ways for young people to relate to their fears and imperfections, allowing them to overcome their anxieties, find peak performance under pressure, and connect deeply with the beauty of their sport.

2. I want parents and coaches to gain a clearer understanding of what the modern athlete endures,

so they can better support their children and players as they deal with such issues as pressure to perform, distractions on their phones, party cultures, and more.

3. And, most importantly, I hope this book inspires both players and coaches to commit to mental training, and specifically meditation. Meditation helps athletes and teams achieve a competitive advantage, and results in happier, more resilient players who are better able to endure the inevitable ups and downs of an athletic career. When mental training is integrated into athletic culture it will also prepare young people to become happier, more productive adults.

First, I tell my story of mental collapse and recovery, highlighting what I learned along the way. Then, to complete the book, I offer advice relevant to athletes, coaches, and parents on how to cultivate successful athletic careers that set up young people for well-lived lives.

"But in the big octagonal hole in the ground with its serrated scalloped concrete sides it was not important, to the spectators, who was fighting, or who would win. It was only important that the winy air and excitement of anticipated conflict be enjoyed, bringing back the distant continent of home where all the grave young highschool athletes who, despite their coaches with their turned-up topcoat collars and conflicting visions of Knut Rockne movies and jobs they feared to risk, fought frantically with the magnificent foolishness of youth as if the whole of life depended on this game, and who were still young enough to cry over a defeat, an illusion that their coaches never shared, a thing that like Santa Claus, they themselves would lose all too soon before the widening range of vision and the knowledge that their loyalty was a commodity and could be shifted easily, and a thing that the men who perched on the concrete of the Boxing Bowl remembered fondly in their own hunger for a return to innocence."

- James Jones, *From Here to Eternity*

CHAPTE

GHOSTY O

1

As with so many kids, sports were ve ... o me during my childhood and adolescen ... shland, Oregon's youth athletic world wasn't perfect, but it was close enough. The local Little League was well funded, affordable, and well run. The YMCA offered soccer, basketball, and flag football leagues. Many parents volunteered their time as coaches and administrators.

I was relatively tall and coordinated, and athletics came naturally. I enjoyed competing with friends from age five on. In elementary school I played baseball, basketball, and rotated between flag and tackle football. Our teams were successful against neighboring towns, and I also enjoyed personal success.

To push myself, I joined leagues with players older than I was. When I was 11 we won the district 12-year-old Little League championship for the first time in over a decade, and we repeated as champions when I was 12. I often dominated in youth basketball, and my early success was both a blessing and a curse—it gave me a sense of confidence and purpose, but also led to an inflated ego.

2

Looking back, I realize that I spent my childhood happily obsessed with sports, often returning to class with grass stains and skinned knees after hard play at recess. Like

kids, I followed professional teams and their
yers and often went to school wearing a Derek Jeter,
ton Manning, or Allen Iverson jersey.

My Dad fostered my love for sports by not turning participation into work. He took me to professional sporting events and stood with me outside stadiums before and after games so I could see and sometimes meet my heroes. We collected sports memorabilia together. He offered positive reinforcement, and instead of pushing me to practice long and hard, he helped me enjoy myself so that practicing hard was my own idea.

I owe much of my early success to the love for sports he cultivated. If games had been too much like work, and if pressure had been applied to me at an early age, I doubt I'd have spent countless hours shooting all alone on my outdoor court, or asking my dad to throw me batting practice until the sun went down at the end of a long summer day.

Another benefit was growing up in a neighborhood where my friends and I were free to play without adult supervision. During the summers we rode our bikes to a local park to spend hours playing Wiffle ball, touch football, basketball, or soccer. We negotiated our own rules as we went and learned to resolve conflicts. The hundreds of hours we spent together, simply having fun, were indispensable to my development as a young athlete.

3

Many (or most) young people find their middle school years challenging, and I was no exception. I was lucky enough to attend a good school, to have close friends, and to enjoy continued athletic success, but I suffered from the normal insecurities. I was so desperate for validation that I needed everyone to know that I was the best athlete around. My lack of confidence must have come across as arrogance.

I wrestled with my own mind. I tried to appear humble, but needed people to know how athletically talented I was. During adolescence, my attitude toward sports morphed from focusing on enjoyment to enhancing my reputation by playing on winning teams and recording impressive statistics. I dreamed about performing well enough at the Division I college level to play professionally after that. Was I as good as current NBA players were when they were in 7th grade? In 8th grade I worried because I couldn't dunk yet. I also wondered whether I'd have a better chance at going pro by specializing in a single sport.

4

My grandfather—to me he's Opa—was a high-level football, basketball, and volleyball player in his day. I was surprised when he told me that when his high school basketball season ended, he didn't touch a ball again until his first practice the following season. He'd show up for basketball a few days after his final football game, and could barely make a free throw. The same was true for football and volleyball—he practiced little, if at all, during off-seasons. As a teenager in Hawaii, he spent summers surfing, spearfishing, dating tourist girls, and being a kid. In other words, he had fun. He explained that enjoying the offseason was no disadvantage athletically, because nobody else in Hawaii was training during off-seasons either, thus creating a level playing field.

Later in his life and far from Hawaii, Opa saw the same relatively low-key state of affairs in both college and professional football. Few, if any, college players lifted weights or worked out during their off-seasons. In the late 1950s, an NFL player in the locker room after practice was likely to light up a cigarette, and so long as he "did his job," the coaches didn't object.

By the time I reached 9th grade, I had coaches from three sports trying to persuade me that I should be focusing on their sport full time and giving up the others. My summers were spent bouncing around between baseball and basketball games, with travel tournaments in each sport, wondering all the while whether I should be playing football. A free day to go wakeboarding with my friends at the lake was a rare and appreciated gift. I felt as if I wasn't training enough for either baseball or basketball, and wondered if I could get good enough in either sport to impress college scouts.

CHAPTER 2

_____

VARSITY

1

By the time I started high school, I'd developed a reputation as a talented player—and an arrogant one. In middle school I'd bragged to classmates that I'd be a varsity player as a freshman, and the boast traveled to high school with me. Upperclassmen didn't like it, so when basketball tryouts began I felt a coldness in the gym. The JV coach seemed to be singling me out with his criticisms, and older players were hostile to me during drills and scrimmages.

When assigned to the JV basketball team with sophomores and juniors, I reigned in my arrogance as best I could. I didn't say much during practice, and worked hard, and was accepted by the other players and the coaching staff. I played well early on and was soon called up to the varsity, where I broke the freshman points-in-a-single-game record and contributed sporadically through the season.

After my successful freshman year of basketball I was placed on the JV2 baseball team. My friend and classmate Ethan was an excellent athlete, and we had a rivalry between us. He made the varsity baseball team as a freshman, and it tormented me that I was left behind. After the intensity of varsity basketball games, JV2 baseball felt like a waste of time. I thought about quitting, but ended up glad I didn't.

2

My goal as a sophomore in basketball was to play in the rotation and contribute, and I exceeded my expectations. I found a rhythm on offense early and often, scored 24 points in the first half of a preseason game, finished the year as the team's leading scorer, and was named to the all-conference first team.

We won our conference and earned a home playoff game to determine who would qualify for the state tournament in Eugene. The day before our big game I was featured in a front-page article in the local paper titled "Hansen 'The Real Deal'". Two quotes from the article:

> "Hansen, sophomore or not, can do more than just handle pressure. He seems to thrive on it."

> "Ashland High boys basketball coach Larry Kellems remembers the night Billy Hansen the sophomore upstart emerged as Billy Hansen the all-star caliber, cold-blooded-shooting go-to player."

With the home gym packed for the game, my blood was anything but cold. I was intensely nervous, and it hurt my performance. After missing my first five shots I felt fearful and useless on the court. I didn't want the ball and finished the game going 0 for 8 and pointless in a three point loss. I felt devastated for letting the seniors down, and embarrassed that so many people had seen me fail in the biggest game of the season. The performance should have made me try to understand what had happened to me and why, but I forced the embarrassing performance out of my mind and moved ahead to baseball.

In my first varsity game I went 4-4 including a triple and a homerun, which sparked a successful season. I was named second team all-state first baseman and posted one of the highest batting averages in the state. We had a talented team, and made it to the state championship game, where we were shut out by Andrew Moore, who went on to pitch at Oregon State and then in the major leagues.

Nervous again, I went 0-3 against Moore—and again did my best to forget about my low level of play under pressure. But problems can't be solved by pretending they don't exist.

3

As a sophomore I went through a rite of passage experienced by millions of teenagers every year. I'd never been drunk, and some upper-classmen friends convinced me to attend my first high school party. They picked me up from home and—the old story—we headed toward a student's house whose parents were gone for the weekend.

Inside the front door was a dimly lit room with loud music thumping and upper-classmen standing in groups holding large red plastic cups. The pungent smell of pot smoke was pervasive. I followed my friends through the living room and out the back door, where some teammates and classmates were standing by a fire and drinking. My first appearance at a party brought friends across the yard to greet me—some with red cheeks and glossed-over eyes, whose breaths smelled sweet and somehow sinister. My best friend since elementary school dragged me back into the kitchen for my first shot of vodka. Luckily there was orange juice available to wash the harsh taste out of my mouth.

After a few shots I wandered around, feeling more uncomfortable than I ever had on a basketball court or baseball field. While no one else seemed to have problems blending in with the crowd, I had no idea where to stand or what to say. I stuck close to my friends and had a few more shots. When I left, I decided that partying wasn't for me.

Based on that experience I took a stance against alcohol and drugs that lasted through high school. When my friends nagged me about not going to parties, I told them I was committed to athletics and didn't want to ruin my chances of playing in college. But looking back, I realize that avoiding the party scene had more to do with my social anxieties than it did with a commitment to sports.

I'm not sorry that I waited until college to start partying. It's common knowledge that teenagers don't do much of anything in moderation, and that drugs and alcohol can cause long-term harm to the adolescent brain and body. I had teammates and friends who partied hard every weekend. A few of them showed up stoned to school and practice and suffered in both academics and sports because of it. The possible downside to my puritanical high school days is that it might have set the stage for my abuse of alcohol in college.

4

"Vronsky, meanwhile, in spite of the complete realization of what he so long desired, was not perfectly happy. He soon felt that the realization of his desires gave him no more than a grain of sand out of the mountain of happiness he had expected. It showed

**him the mistake men make in picturing to themselves
happiness as the realization of their desires."**

- Leo Tolstoy, Anna Karenina

If someone had guaranteed me before my sophomore year began that I'd lead the basketball team in scoring and be named the second best first baseman in the state, I'd have been elated, certain that my wellbeing and happiness would drastically improve. But as that year unfolded, my expectations changed along with my circumstances. Instead of enjoying my success, I worried about it disappearing, and looked toward an uncertain future with anxiety.

In the summer after my sophomore baseball season, our Legion baseball team won the state tournament and advanced to the regionals in Montana. Ashland had won state before, but never regionals, so our obvious goal was to win it for the first time.

We stayed together in a barn converted into living quarters in rural Montana, and drove vans into town for each game. The week was pressure-packed and exciting. In the double-elimination tournament we won four of our first five games and made it to the championship game against a team with a star pitcher. The night before the big game we had an emotional team gathering, and, full of nervous anticipation, all of us had trouble sleeping. I'd played well so far, and was fixated on helping Ashland win its first regional championship. If that happened, I was sure I'd be happy for a very long time.

Our hot hitting continued, and we enjoyed a comfortable lead throughout the game. After our ace pitcher struck out their final batter, the traditional dog-pile ensued on the mound. Then we posed for pictures with the championship trophy. To make matters even better, from all the teams in Oregon, Washington, Nevada, Idaho, and Montana, I was named the tournament MVP. Maybe nothing's ever perfect, but this seemed as close as anything could get.

I was relatively happy during our celebration, but I was already distracted by intrusive thoughts. How could I use my MVP status to gain the attention of college scouts? What was the best way to post my MVP photo on Facebook?

Later, at the local pizza shop with teammates and parents, I felt somehow disconnected to everyone, and to the moment. Thoughts about how I could leverage the experience obliterated my enjoyment of it, because the beauty of the moment didn't matter all that much if it didn't lead to some later, greater end.

CHAPTER 3

RECRUITED

1

After my sophomore summer baseball season my attention shifted to the recruiting process. Having naively self-defined myself as a "star athlete," I was terrified of the possibility that I wouldn't be offered a college scholarship. It bothered me every single day and often kept me awake at night. I had no clear idea about how well I had to perform to earn a scholarship, and didn't know what level of competition I should be aiming for.

I got lots of advice from parents, coaches, and other adults in my community. Some told me what I hoped was true—that if I was good enough I'd be discovered, even in remote southern Oregon. Others advised me to market myself, which meant sending emails, calling coaches, and going to camps and "showcases."

Many (or most) gifted high school athletes are determined to go "D-1." While playing for any college generally carries prestige, Division I is the top level. The best players on major college football and basketball teams are treated like superheroes, and the reasons are clear: in football and basketball, popular teams appear regularly on nationwide television. Professional teams draft almost exclusively from Division 1, so signing a letter of intent to a D-1 school carries at least the possibility of playing professionally, even though the percentage of D-1 athletes who compete professionally is minuscule.

Most people have no idea how few high schoolers are offered D-1 scholarships. I broke records at Ashland High School, and my baseball teams were in the hunt for state championships every year. This led many community members (teachers, family friends, classmates) to assume that, after signing with a high-powered university, I'd soon be appearing in primetime television games. Their misplaced confidence in me wrongly inflated my expectations.

2

Early on in my junior year basketball season, I sent my highlight tape out along with my statistics and accolades to about 50 Division 1 schools. The tape was a montage of splashed three-pointers from all over the court. I immediately received a flurry of responses, all saying essentially the same thing: "Hi Billy, I'm very interested in you as a potential addition to our team. Could you send full-game film? Thanks, Coach X."

My Dad and I were ecstatic, and I was all but certain that I'd soon be playing at the highest college level. We chose a full-game film in which I scored 36 points including eight 3s, and led a comeback victory against a good team. It had been by far my best performance, and I felt confident each time I hit the send button to a coach.

Then came a crushing silence that lasted for weeks—I didn't receive a single response from any of the coaches who'd requested the game film. Finally I sent a follow up email to each coach, and received a few replies informing me that I wasn't right for their program, and wishing me luck in the future. I hadn't kept my excitement to myself after the first flurry of emails, and had told friends, coaches, and others about the interest I'd received from the likes of University of Portland, Davidson University, Air Force, and other D-1 schools. Now, with my hopes crushed, I had to deal with uncomfortable questions about which school I'd likely sign with.

In hindsight, it's clear that coaches were impressed with my shooting ability, but didn't see me as athletic enough to be a Division I guard.

The only place I knew was Ashland, Oregon, and I had friends, family, female interests, and the local community to impress. My goal of committing to the best possible university had little if anything to do with where my best experience in college might be, and a lot to do with the likes and comments I'd get on Facebook, and what the front page article in the *Ashland Tidings* would say about me, and how my community would respond. That's what infected me with the D-1 virus.

CHAPTER 4

FALLING OUT OF BOUNDS

1

As a high school junior my basketball team had far less talent than the year prior, and I found myself in charge of the offense. I began every game wanting to help us win, but I thought about my scoring average, and what it would take to be noticed by college scouts. When we struggled, I often lost trust in my teammates and tried to take games over. Sometimes this led to come-from-behind wins, but just as often I left games feeling frustrated and guilty for missing too many shots. I averaged about 18 points per game, but took too many shots to get there.

There were high points, like hitting a falling-out-of-bounds game winner against our conference rivals. We all enjoyed ourselves on bus trips and in the locker room. But our season ended early with a first round playoff loss, and I still hadn't received the attention I craved from college scouts. I began thinking that baseball could be my path.

2

I never knew exactly what my shooting percentages were in high school basketball. For whatever reason, stats weren't available to players. If I shot 6 for 22 the paper would print that "Hansen led the Grizzlies with 18 points, and three 3-pointers." It's possible that the coach didn't want his players worrying about their stats.

Some of my darkest moments as a baseball player related to personal statistics. During my junior year season it was a foregone conclusion that we'd win our conference, and we entered the state playoffs with 25 wins and a single defeat. Because there'd been no doubt about winning our conference, our focus all season long was on the only dramatic elements left: Who would end up with the best numbers? Who would make the all-conference team, the all-state team? Who had a chance to finish the season batting over .500?

I had a running total of my hits and at-bats firmly in mind, and I spent class periods generating hypothetical scenarios with my calculator. If I go 1 for 8 in Saturday's doubleheader, how far down will my batting average go? What if I go 4-8? How many hits do I need per game, on average, to break the school record? These distractions translated to the field. After hitting a rocket line drive straight to the shortstop, I felt devastated. If I fisted a pathetic blooper over the first baseman's head, I reached first base elated. Much of my mood in the dugout and on defense was determined by how I was hitting in that particular game or stretch of games. Instead of focusing on what I could control, I was strictly results-oriented. Only a close, intense game could transcend my personal worries, and these games, in which winning was more important than anything else, produced enjoyable competitive experiences.

My analytical, over-thinking nature probably elevated my stats obsession to unusual extremes, but I'm certain that this experience is shared to some degree by most athletes. If you watch the NBA closely enough, occasionally you'll see a player dribbling the ball toward the half-court line with two or three seconds left in a quarter, and he'll wait until the horn goes off before flinging the ball toward the hoop. He's creating the illusion that he tried to score, but he was really protecting his shooting percentage by avoiding an almost certain miss. One of my close friends in college admitted to a skill he'd developed: making a quick extra pass at the end of the shot clock to force someone else to take the desperation heave, which was almost always a miss.

On September 28, 1941, Boston Red Sox star Ted Williams admirably chose to risk his chance at achieving a remarkable statistical goal. It was the last day of the season and Williams was batting .400 going into a doubleheader against the Philadelphia Athletics. The games would have no effect on the final standings, and Red Sox manager Joe Cronin told Williams that, if he wanted, he could sit the games out and protect his batting average. Williams not only turned the offer down, he felt insulted that Cronin had made the suggestion, and he played both games, went 6 for 8, maintained his self-respect, and raised his average to .406.

3

Situation 1: In the second game of a meaningless doubleheader—we had an eight run lead late in the game—both the team and our fans in attendance were disengaged. I was having a subpar day at the plate and had been taken out of the game so my backup could get some at-bats. I was slumped over on the dugout bench, frustrated about how poorly I'd hit the ball, and, as usual, preoccupied with my batting average. How far had it dropped? My friend Ethan was still in the game and he was on fire. Brent, Ethan, and I were all hitting around .500 for the season, and one of us would win the conference batting title. When Ethan came to the plate I watched intently, secretly hoping he'd make an out. He put a bad swing on an inside fastball and fisted a weak fly ball into shallow center field. There was indecision on the center fielder's part, and confusion between the shortstop and second basemen, ending with all three of them giving up on the ball, which dropped softly onto the outfield grass. As the ball landed I let out an involuntary "Fuck!" under my breath, and then nervously looked around the dugout to make sure nobody had heard me. I was relieved that my dark intentions remained a secret.

Situation 2: On a hot July day we faced Roseberg in the legion semifinals. We'd battled back from a deficit and trailed by one run in the top of the last inning. Everybody—players, coaches, fans, and umpires—had been totally engaged in the game on every pitch. I came to the plate with one out and a runner on second base. Overanxious to make something happen, I chased a slider on the outside corner and popped up to the first baseman. My poor at-bat would normally have bothered me until my next at-bat, but by the time I got back to the dugout, my attention was focused on Ethan, who followed me in the batting order. He was a slow base runner, and the most dangerous power hitter on the field, so, with two outs and a runner on second, he likely wouldn't see anything good to hit. With a 2-0 count, the pitcher made the conservative choice and broke off a curveball, which Ethan had been waiting for. He launched a towering fly ball deep over the left field fence. As soon as the ball left the bat I was airborne over the dugout fence, letting out a roar of joy, feeling nothing but gratitude for my friend's success, and for our one run lead late in the game. My mind had been clearly focused on our collective goal, free from worry about my own perceived status.

Even before I'd done any serious self-analysis or mental training, I remember being aware of how much more enjoyable my state of mind was in situation two. Big games and big moments in sports have the power to transcend concerns about stats and status within a team. In these moments, we lose ourselves in the game and forget entirely about our own batting averages and scoring percentages. Our friends' and teammates' successes aren't a cause for envy, but a reason to celebrate.

This begs an important question: is a constructive state of mind available only in pressure-packed competitions with major implications, or can it also occur in ordinary situations?

4

Even in high school I knew what it meant "to have my mind right" before or during competition. Sometimes I felt stifled, timid, envious, angry, or sluggish. Other times I felt calm and focused, and I'd forget everything except the game itself. Even as I exerted maximum effort I felt relaxed and centered. I also knew what it was like to be "in the zone," when I felt like I could do no wrong.

This is a common phenomenon in sports, music, poetry, mathematics and other difficult disciplines. Mihaly Csikszentmihalyi, a Hungarian-American psychologist, studied these states of consciousness and coined the term "flow state," describing "flow" as "being completely involved in an activity for its own sake. The ego falls away. Time flies. Every action, movement, and thought follows inevitably from the previous one, like playing jazz. Your whole being is involved, and you're using your skills to the utmost." In his work, Csikszentmihalyi claims that flow is the result of the correct balance between the challenge of the task and the skill of the performer, and that both must be high. When a highly skilled performer gives full effort and concentration to a difficult task, a flow state can result.

Jamie Wheal and Steven Kotler studied the phenomena of flow and altered states of consciousness in *Stealing Fire*, and define flow as an "Optimal state of consciousness where we feel our best and perform our best. Flow refers to those 'in the zone' moments, where focus gets so intense that everything else disappears. Action and awareness start to merge. Our sense of self vanishes, our sense of time as well, and all aspects of performance, both physical and mental, go through the roof." When immersed in this state, all thought about time, score, and context drops away, and only the game remains.

Bill Russell describes his experience of being in "flow" in his memoir *Second Wind*:

> "Every so often a Celtics game would heat up so that it became more than a physical or even mental game, and would be magical. That feeling is difficult to describe, and I certainly never talked about it when I was playing. When it happened, I could feel my play rise to a new level. It came rarely, and

would last anywhere from five minutes to a whole quarter, or more. Three or four plays were not enough to get it going. It would surround not only me and the other team, and even the referees. At that special level, all sorts of odd things happened: The game would be in the white heat of competition, and yet somehow I wouldn't feel competitive, which is a miracle in itself. I'd be putting out the maximum effort, straining, coughing up parts of my lungs as we ran, and yet I never felt the pain. The game would move so quickly that every fake, cut, and pass would be surprising, and yet nothing could surprise me. It was almost as if we were playing in slow motion. During those spells, I could almost sense how the next play would develop and where the next shot would be taken. Even before the other team brought the ball inbounds, I could feel it so keenly that I'd want to shout to my teammates, 'it's coming there!'—except that I knew everything would change if I did. My premonitions would be consistently correct, and I always felt then that I not only knew all the Celtics by heart, but also all the opposing players, and that they all knew me. There have been many times in my career when I felt moved or joyful, but these were the moments when I had chills pulsing up and down my spine."

I never reached the skill level or the resulting flow state that the great Bill Russell describes, but I can relate his description to my best moments on the court. In high school these especially positive states of mind were uncommon and random. Early on in my college career my mind was so disoriented that I actually forgot that such moments existed. It was only after serious mental training that I consistently experienced them on the court.

5

Our junior year baseball team suffered our second loss of the season in the state quarterfinals. We finished the year 27-2, without a championship to show for it. I ended the season batting .544, best in the state, and broke my high school's batting average, hits, runs, and doubles record. But I still wasn't receiving any scholarship offers, and I wondered what I could possibly do to attract the attention of college scouts.

After my junior year season I was selected to play for southern Oregon's elite summer baseball team, the Medford Mustangs. The team consisted of the region's best high school players along with some who had returned from their first year of college. I thought this would be my best chance yet to attract attention.

When I showed up for the first day of practice I was uncomfortable in the new environment. I'd been the biggest fish on my high school teams, and now felt restrained around my new teammates and coaches. Due to my high school stats, I was named as the starting first baseman and placed second in the batting order, between Colin Sowers, a D-1 outfielder, and Seth Brown, who's now playing for the Oakland As.

Batting second made me anxious, and I started the summer poorly. Craving the respect of teammates and coaches, I put too much pressure on myself, and my hitting slump continued. I was dropped from second to seventh in the batting order. A month prior, I'd stepped up to the plate with confidence, certain that when I got a good pitch I'd square it up. Now it felt as if the bat had no sweet spot. My swing felt slow and jerky, and hitting the ball hard was a rare, lucky surprise.

By mid-season I was bouncing in and out of the line-up and starting only against favorable pitching match-ups. A few college scouts I'd made connections with in high school came to watch my games, sometimes showing up to learn that I wasn't even in the line-up.

When we made the state championship game I was given the start against a left-handed pitcher. We lost, and I finished 0-4 with two strikeouts. The whole summer should have served as a red flag for me, another clear indication that I needed to work on the mental aspects of competition. But, again, I did my best to forget about baseball, and looked ahead toward senior year basketball.

CHAPTER 5

LETTER OF INTENT

1

I'd been thinking about my senior year of varsity basketball since elementary school. I was the team's ball boy, so I felt the tense energy of a locker room on game night at a young age. The strong, buttery smell of cheap popcorn blended perfectly with the horns of the school band. Gym rattling chants of "D-FENCE" came from students, cheerleaders, and the small town crowd, giving energy and encouragement to the brave young men who I couldn't wait to be someday. I spent many hours as a young boy alone on my outdoor court imagining myself wearing the Grizzly uniform, knocking down big shots in the hometown gym.

But my Senior year lacked what I'd lived most of my life hoping for. Perhaps this is always true to some extent. A 5th grader views varsity players as superheroes, then grows up and realizes that he and his friends have no superpowers, and in fact still resemble children in many ways.

But there were other factors involved. We had a brand new gym that was somehow much nicer and yet also worse than the old one. Imagine a family that owns a struggling business and finally catches a huge break, allowing them to move from a too-small old house into something presumably much nicer, only to sadly realize that the coziness and warmth they had taken for granted in their old place was gone. Upgrades to old stadiums and arenas often produce this effect.

The state of Oregon had reorganized athletic conferences, ending traditional rivalries that had created a link between current teams and teams past. There had been something romantic about hearing a local community member say, "We've got South tonight," meaning a game against South Medford, a team we had learned to both hate and respect. Now we began competing against teams from three hours away that nobody had ever known of or cared about.

2

I had a great statistical senior season, averaging about 22 points per game, the best in the state. Along with many three-point shooting records, I broke records for points in a game, points in a season, and points in a career. But our team's performance was underwhelming, and sometimes I sensed my teammates' resentment for all the shots I took, and for so many of our set plays being run for me. And my three-point shot didn't feel quite right. My left hand—my guide hand—was too involved, and my shooting form didn't always feel smooth. I'd been advertising myself as a lights out shooter when I contacted college coaches, but now I wondered if I'd scored so many points only because I'd shot too often.

There were exciting moments and competitive games with my friends that temporarily transcended my personal problems. But even after my best game—39 points including ten three-pointers—I couldn't be certain that any scouts had noticed. Alex Young, the point guard for neighboring Phoenix High School, was the only player better than I was in the Rogue Valley. He committed to U. C. Irvine in his junior year and would go on to enjoy an outstanding career there. We'd been friendly rivals for years, and it tormented me that he'd received a Division 1 scholarship as a junior. I'd always compared my success to his, and I was jealous. Now, thinking back to some of my high school teammates who showed up every day and worked hard, only to ride the bench, I feel ashamed. I was fixated on the one player in the valley who was better than me. If they were aware of my petty frustrations, they must have resented them, for good reason.

3

"Never ask while you are doing it if what you are doing is fun."

- Christopher Hitchens, Hitch 22

The night before Senior Night and my final home game, I drove alone to Ashland High School at 10 p.m. I walked into the empty gym and took a seat at the top of the bleachers. Then I went down to sit on the bench looking out at the court. My idea was to experience a moment of reflection before my last game in my home gym. I'd read about other athletes doing that. I hoped someone would walk in and see me sitting alone. After a half minute or so, I pulled out my phone to take a photo, and then typed out a sentimental message about my final game, posted it on Facebook, and left the gym to meet up with some friends.

I was sorry to see my final high school basketball season end, and, looking back, it's clear to me that I mistakenly felt that in order to make my last game matter, I had to create a powerful emotional context for it. I tried to manufacture something memorable instead of simply giving a meaningful moment a chance to happen.

So I played on Senior Night affected by contrived emotion and nostalgia. I shot poorly from the field and scored nine points. In an attempt to salvage the night I tried to dunk on a fast break, but the ball careened off the rim, which might have cost us the game. We lost by one point.

A few nights later we were eliminated in our first playoff game. After the game, my teammates and I were emotional, but I admitted to myself that what I was really doing was manufacturing sadness in an attempt to show that I cared. Others were doing the same thing. Teammates who had told me they were glad to get the season over with pretended to cry, because they knew it was expected.

Many truths are timeless, and here's Nikolenka describing my 21st century reaction perfectly in Leo Tolstoy's first novel, *Childhood, Boyhood and Youth,* written in 1856:

> "I despised myself for not experiencing exclusively a feeling of sorrow and endeavored to conceal all other feelings, and this made my grief insincere and unnatural. Moreover, I derived a kind of pleasure from knowing that I was unhappy and tried to sharpen my sense of unhappiness, and this selfish feeling did more than anything else to smother real sorrow in me."

4

My dad helped me throughout the recruiting process. He traveled to all of my games and filmed them, and then spent countless hours editing highlight tapes. He spearheaded the effort of contacting coaches, collaborating with me in the process. Even with all his help I was overwhelmed. The process of contacting recruiters is haphazard and stressful. We collected emails from college websites and sent out emails with videos embedded. We paid for expensive camps and showcases that felt something like Amway pyramid schemes. Though we established a few connections, we never felt satisfied and never seemed to be doing enough.

After my junior year my dad finally purchased a reputable, and fairly expensive recruiting service called *Student Athlete Showcase*. They set up a sports portfolio webpage with relevant information about me. They kept in close contact regarding emails, and when follow-up emails should be sent, and when coaches should be called to maximize the chance of establishing a connection. More importantly, they asked me what I wanted from my overall college experience.

We purchased the recruiting service in the hopes of receiving a college scholarship. But what we didn't expect was the psychological relief that came with the product. With experts handling the recruiting game plan, I was freed up to focus on performance and enjoying my senior season.

I've learned since then that many recruiting services lead people on and take advantage of desperate athletes, so it's necessary to do research and reject the often inflated claims made by opportunistic marketers.

5

With the help of a recruiting service, I got some serious attention from various Division 2 schools and set up official visits for the spring. The fact that I was a two-sport athlete made my situation unusual. I didn't want to quit either sport and had no way of knowing which one offered better possibilities. I also had to decide if I should accept a D-2 offer, or play for a junior college where I could hopefully develop and keep my D-1 dream alive.

My first of five scheduled visits was to Regis University in Denver, a member of the Rocky Mountain Athletic Conference. My Dad and I arrived at the campus on a bright summer day and were immediately struck by the beautiful red brick buildings and blossoming trees. Friendly coaches showered me with praise, and the players I met were friendly and welcoming. Through the weekend I was treated to delicious meals. The Regis head coach was Lonnie Porter, who had been an excellent player and eventually became a Colorado coaching legend. I was struck by his strong presence. He offered me a full scholarship, worth well over $40,000 per year for four years. Although Regis had struggled in recent years, he assured my Dad and me that we'd win if I decided to come to Regis.

My Dad asked Coach Porter if I'd have to give up baseball if I took the scholarship. Coach Porter reached out to the baseball coach, who viewed my highlight tape, statistics and accolades, and offered me a roster position on the baseball team.

The offer was exciting, and I was ready to see the recruiting process end. I saw myself at Ashland High School answering questions about where and why I'd signed, when I should have been asking myself if I'd be able to play two sports that overlap and still have time to do well in my classes. And I should have gone on my remaining visits and compared my options.

Instead, I anticipated the praise I'd get back home after signing to play two sports. I canceled the remaining visits, a lengthy feature story appeared in the Ashland Tidings, and I proudly wore a Regis hat on my high school campus.

Chapter 6

IMPOSTER

1

After an emotional day and night saying goodbye to friends and family, I boarded my flight to Denver with my mom and dad. Mom helped me set up my dorm room. Saying goodbye to my parents, knowing I wouldn't see them again for months, wasn't easy. I realized for the first time how much my life had changed.

Some of my older friends who'd played in college warned me that coaches who'd pampered and praised them during recruiting weren't nearly as friendly after the paperwork had been signed. When I showed up at the Regis gym for the first time I was relieved when Coach Daniels greeted me with the same warmth and respect he'd shown me when we first met in Ashland.

But I felt nervous walking with him into the locker room. Coach Daniels is tall and lanky. He has a sharp basketball mind and an infectious personality. He showed me my nameplate above a locker and explained locker room etiquette, emphasizing that Coach Porter was strict about the rules. Then he asked in his usual friendly tone, "You want to do some shooting before we check out the cafeteria?"

He probably expected me to say yes, but I felt a surge of anxiety and muttered something like, "I'll come back when I have a little more time."

He nodded, and as we left the gym I felt relief.

I know now that when that happened I'd already become a victim of imposter syndrome. Somewhere in my subconscious was the idea that I'd "snuck" my way onto the team, and that if I shot in front of Coach he'd wonder whether he'd made a mistake by offering me a scholarship. The slight hitch in my shot hadn't gone away—somehow my left hand was too involved with my release, and it only got worse with nervousness.

That scholarship I'd boasted about to friends and family back in Oregon now felt like something difficult to live up to. I'd spent years putting $10 at a time in my gas tank and hunting for lunch specials so I could save my allowance. Was I really worth $44,000 per year?

This dynamic is surprisingly common. Renee Pirkl, a sports psychologist who works with Pac-12 and NBA basketball teams, told me that many of the players she deals with feel like imposters—that the other players on the team deserve to be there, but they've somehow snuck into the party.

I knew nothing about this as a college freshman, and for as long as I could manage it, I tried to avoid playing in front of the coaches. But of course I had to play in front of them, and every time I did I left the gym creating stories in my mind about what they might be saying about me behind closed doors. In my mind I'd already become a failure.

2

The basketball team held an optional open gym on the Friday before school started. My new teammates had been welcoming enough during my visit, and now it was like the locker rooms I was familiar with, complete with freewheeling jokes and playful insults.

The locker room talk soon shifted to that night's parties. The other freshmen and I were told the address of a house on campus where a "pre-game" (the drinking before a house party, reserved for those on the team) would start at 8 o'clock sharp. My partying experience was limited, and my plan for college was to remain mostly sober due to my athletic commitment.

But the upperclassmen commanded respect, and I wanted to make a good first impression.

I showed up at the pre-game address 15 minutes early and was immediately offered a bottle of Burnett's pineapple vodka. My teammates stared straight at me to see what I'd do, so I tipped the bottle back and took a big mouthful of cheap vodka that burned my throat as I struggled to swallow it down.

"Fuck yeah, this kid can party!" somebody said.

I understood how to fit into my new environment.

3

In high school I'd been faster and more athletic than my teammates and opponents, so I showed up to practices and games with more than enough confidence. My wake-up call at Regis was watching the other guards on the team smash windmill dunks during warm-ups. These were players from places like Texas, Southern California, and Arizona.

I'd liked and respected my high school coaches, but their level of intensity was nothing like what I experienced at Regis. Having rarely faced serious criticism, I was totally unprepared for Coach Porter. When I arrived he was entering his 35th season as the Head Coach. Despite his worn out knees, which made him grimace as he moved, he seemed younger than his age, and he turned out to be an honorable man who demanded respect. Even though many of us mocked his coaching style behind his back, we all sought his approval.

But he was furiously intense and demanding on the court, so even though much of his criticism was valid, the threat of getting yelled at was intimidating, and I responded poorly to the new pressure.

My lack of defensive training created a major problem. Six-three is relatively tall in high school, so I often guarded forwards, and sometimes even "bigs." In college I had a hard time staying in front of guards who were my size and faster than me.

I wasn't prepared to play effectively in the RMAC, and should have been benched or redshirted my freshman season. I found myself in the playing rotation because Regis had been 2-20 in conference play the year before; they wanted to invest in the new talent, in the hopes that we could turn things around. In our first game I started strong against a team from a lower division, scoring 15 points including some three-pointers. Then, when tougher competition came, my weaknesses were exposed.

4

The high school competition I was used to had been sped up by about 50%. What had been enough space to shoot from in high school wasn't enough anymore, and many of my shots were blocked or altered. I was bullied in the paint by bigger, stronger, faster guards. As the season progressed, my confidence evaporated.

As this happened I adopted the drinking habits of my teammates. Our games were on Friday and Saturday nights, and every Saturday night I got drunk. By mid-season I felt tired and rundown both physically and mentally, and I spent more and more time on the bench.

Still in the hunt for a playoff spot late in January, we hosted Adams State for a crucial match-up. We battled them to the very end, but found ourselves in desperation mode with less than a minute remaining. I was in the game because we needed three-pointers to make up ground. Down by 4 with time winding down, Kevin, our point guard, knocked down a wild three-pointer. We moved into a frantic press to try to get a steal, which left us exposed over the top. The inbounder threw a football pass down the court and connected with his man, who (stupidly) rose up to dunk the ball. Out of timeouts, and down three with only seconds remaining, we were in panic mode. The ball was inbounded to me under our own basket. Sensing my defender (stupidly) running toward me, I moved into him as I flung the ball toward the rim at the opposite baseline. As I watched the ball fall far short of our basket, the screech of the whistle sounded in unison with the final buzzer. The three-point shooting foul the referee called threw the Adams State bench into a wild protest.

My first thought was, "Oh no… I have to make three straight free throws to send this into overtime." I looked toward our bench and I can still remember Coach Daniels clapping and saying, "Good job," but his eyes told me he had no more confidence than I did.

Approaching the free throw line, my heart was pounding and my vision seemed to blur. I tried to refocus my attention as I caught the ball from the referee. The opposing players were peppering me with insults: "Don't worry about it, he'll choke." "Look at him, he's shaking already." I went into my routine, and nervously released my first shot. It bounced on the front rim, hit the backboard, spun around the hoop and finally fell in. I hadn't prayed in years, but I remember thinking, "Maybe God is going to help me do this." I touched hands with teammates while teammates and coaches yelled encouragement from the bench.

I caught the ball from the referee again, and began my dribbling routine. As I bent my knees to go into my shot, I heard a vicious voice from behind me saying "Pressure busts pipes, motherfucker!" This release felt better than my first one. I watched the ball glide towards the basket, rattle inside the hoop and pop out—game over.

After the game, Coach Porter addressed me in front of the team, emphatically telling me not to beat myself up about the missed free throw. He even caught up with me before I left the gym to make sure I was okay before going home. My teammates encouraged me not to stress about it. I was thankful for everyone's support, but still felt about as miserable as I'd ever felt anywhere. Under the shower in my dorm room, with my head pressed against the wall, tears fell into the running water.

5

We missed the playoffs by a few games. I played an average of 14 minutes in all 25 games and finished the season shooting a dismal 31% from the floor, 24% from the three point line, and 47% from the free throw line. By any standards, it had been a miserable season. I felt as if I'd been tossed into the deep end of a pool and didn't know how to swim.

By the time basketball ended the baseball team had already played eight preseason games, and had established team dynamics and chemistry. Meanwhile, I hadn't touched a bat in months. In my first practice my swing felt slow and my throwing arm weak. I had trouble assimilating into the team because many of them treated me as an outsider.

The coach recommended that I redshirt. My swing didn't come around until a couple of weeks before the season ended, and I spent every practice impatiently waiting for it to end. Trying to do well in two sports seemed hopeless, so I gave up baseball to concentrate on salvaging my basketball career.

6

What had happened? When I opened my eyes I found myself on the floor, in the narrow canyon between my bed and my roommate's bed, my clothes and the floor smeared with vomit. The smell was awful.

I checked my phone. Multiple texts from a volleyball player asked if I was okay. I texted her yes and asked what had happened to me. She explained that she'd stayed with me most of the night and taken care of me while I shivered and vomited. A boy on my floor had seen my legs sticking out of a bathroom stall like a dead body. Inside the stall he found me face down and passed out. Knowing that an RA would take me to detox if he found me, which would circle back to my coaches, he and a friend dragged me back to my room and then texted the volleyball player, because they'd seen me with her earlier. Because I was shivering and dry heaving, she'd almost decided to take me to the emergency room.

I didn't remember any of this, and all I felt was guilt and shame. I'd completed a transition from a self-assured, committed athlete to a pathetic, self-destructive drunk, a burden to my friends and classmates.

I thanked and apologized profusely to everyone involved, and I bought them gifts for their help. I looked forward to home. I was an underperforming athlete without an academic direction, but with a drinking problem.

CHAPTER 7

THE SPIRAL

1

It was a relief to escape Regis and the pressure to perform, but as soon as my Oregon summer began I started worrying about it ending. Without an organized plan, my summer training was erratic. I worked hard on the court and in the weight room, but my momentum was often interrupted by family trips and by too many opportunities to drink too much.

Whenever I left town on a family trip, or to go camping or to a ball game, I worried about the workouts I was missing, and when I did work out I felt unsatisfied with my progress. Sometimes I left the gym furious at my mediocre shooting. My mom is a teacher at an elementary school in Ashland, and she'd sometimes give me the key so I could go shoot late at night. Once, after missing consecutive free throws, I punted the ball so hard that I put a hole in the gym ceiling. How did I become so enraged?

August 23rd came on like a storm cloud. I lost sleep in the nights leading up to my return to Regis.

2

Back in Denver things started decently. My coaches noticed the muscle I'd put on in the weight room during the summer, and I played well in our first couple of open gyms. There was an enjoyable buzz around the team, a honeymoon phase common in team sports, when players, coaches, and fans all share an optimistic view of how the coming season will likely unfold.

But my optimism soon began to fade. After a few subpar practices, a couple of embarrassing air balls, and being yelled at a few times by my coach, I was back to constant worry about underperforming. I don't remember any single moment that zapped my confidence in shooting the ball. Instead, it was as if my confidence tank had sprung a slow leak, and over the course of weeks the tank was drained. I didn't know how to deal with unkind criticism and tried to hide my insecurities from the coaching staff.

My anxiety on the court increased. I'd been nervous before, causing me to play tentatively and ineffectually, but never before had the simplest acts become challenging. I felt a numbing tension in my hands, chest, and face, making every movement feel unnatural. My mind seemed to freeze and I felt waves of nausea. As bad as my freshman year had been, this one was worse.

3

I had no way of anticipating the depression and paralyzing performance anxiety that would afflict me at about midseason. But, looking back, I realize that my mind was developing the necessary prerequisites for that outcome. I thought about upcoming practices and workouts incessantly, and became intensely nervous before every practice. Desperate to have a good season, and trying to apply advice from self-help coaches on YouTube, I accepted the premise that in order to achieve success I'd have to work tirelessly and make every conceivable sacrifice.

Hoping to gain an advantage over my teammates and to generate confidence, I started making outrageous commitments to myself about how I'd live. For example, I decided that stopping drinking and partying altogether would solve my basketball problems.

One Friday night the team was organizing our "pre-game" in a group conversation. We had practice the next morning at 8:30, and I'd promised myself a good night's sleep. While all my friends were out enjoying themselves, I stayed home alone and did my best to rest and relax, hoping to outperform them at practice. But instead of getting enough sleep, I lost sleep worrying first about missing out on the party—would one of my friends hook up with the girl I liked?—and then about how practice would go after a sleepless night.

I showed up at practice early and did my best to appear fresh in front of my coaches. When my hungover teammates came out of the locker room onto the court I was already practicing three-point shots.

For a while my sacrifice paid off. I completed the ball handling and defensive drills with purpose and speed while my teammates merely went through the motions. But once we divided up for the scrimmage, my anxiety returned. I ended up guarding a close friend who'd partied especially hard the night before. As I fought through screens and chased him on defense I could smell the alcohol in his sweat, but he found space and knocked down shots. On offense I was unassertive and missed the few shots I took.

Frustrated and desperate, I pressured him to keep him from shooting over me. But all it took was a simple jab fake for him to drive around me and gain the advantage. When I sprinted to cut him off he hit me with a step back move. When I lost my balance he made the shot, and then trash talked me loudly enough so that everybody could hear it. My desperation turned into rage.

When I pressured him a few possessions later I got a hand on a pass and deflected the ball toward half court. We both chased hard, but he had the advantage again, so I impulsively shoved him to the floor with both hands. I'll never forget the look of shock and disgust he gave me.

Coach rightly yelled at me, and told us not to guard each other anymore. At that point I felt like crying. I'd done "everything right" by not going out and trying to get enough rest, and my hungover friend outplayed me anyway.

Later in the locker room spirits were high as we were cutting off our ankle tape and changing out of our practice gear, as this was the last practice of the week. I tried not to sulk while everyone around me joked and laughed, sharing stories about the fun they'd had the night before. I don't remember ever feeling like more of a loser.

I went out that night and drank too much with my friends.

4

The most debilitating symptom of my anxiety was how un-natural the basketball felt in my hands. Whenever I held it, everything seemed wrong. Gripping the ball with stiff, uncooperative fingers led me to awkwardly cock my wrist so as to get it directly behind the ball. But the ball spun off my guide hand in unreliable and unpredictable ways. The more anxious I became, the more my left hand got involved with the shot. I could barely remember how it felt to shoot easily and cleanly.

I felt that my teammates and coaches were watching me with either pity or disappointment. In our customary full court weave shooting drill that began practice, I'd sometimes bounce wide-open mid-range jump shots off the backboard. I occasionally shot airballs from the free throw line. With every free throw my heart raced and I held my breath. When I hit the rim I was relieved.

My troubles on the court bled into other areas of life. It became almost impossible to enjoy anything, because no matter what I did, the next practice or game was rapidly approaching. Sitting in class or eating in the cafeteria with friends, I counted down the hours. My only moments of relative peace came directly after a practice or game in which I hadn't embarrassed myself.

I also found some temporary relief in being asleep, so I spent much of my free time lying in bed trying to nap, even when I wasn't tired. Two hours of escape from everything seemed precious. But in compensation for afternoon naps, I sometimes stayed up far too late at night, eating junk food while watching episode after episode of mindless TV.

Finally, I decided to see the sports psychologist on campus.

5

"Let me tell ya something. Nowadays, everybody's gotta go to shrinks, and counselors, and go on Sally Jessy Raphael and talk about their problems. What happened to Gary Cooper? The strong, silent type. That was an American."

- Tony Soprano

At the Student Health Office I was worried that someone I knew would enter and see me making an appointment. My mental struggles were a closely guarded secret. NBA forward Gordon Hayward spoke of his own resistance to seeing a therapist as he worked his way back from a devastating ankle injury: "It's hard," he said. "It's embarrassing. You want to be the guy that says, 'I'm strong. I don't need any help.'" I shared this standard male mindset—that seeking help from an outsider was soft and pathetic.

I met with a woman named Jeni Shannon. I got the immediate impression that she was a compassionate, trustworthy and serious person. She assured me that everything was confidential, and that my coaches and teammates wouldn't know I'd been there. I did my best to explain to her what I was going through. It was the first time I'd described the situation clearly to anyone, including myself. Revealing the details forced me to contend with the seriousness of my problem.

After a few meetings she told me I was suffering from performance anxiety and depression. Although I knew she was right, hearing the words shocked me. It was difficult to accept where I'd ended up.

6

In his helpful, harrowing book *Darkness Visible,* William Styron described his struggles. The depression that Styron experienced was exponentially worse than what I dealt with. In fact, I feel guilty for having been depressed in circumstances that many people might regard as a form of heaven: I was young and healthy, on a full scholarship at an excellent university to play basketball with my friends. But the pain and anguish I experienced were real, and all-important to me at the time. My entire sophomore year has the character of a nightmare that, described the next day, feels trivial. But it was traumatic and debilitating when I experienced it.

The two states of mind I experienced (as described by Styron) were confusion and hopelessness. For reasons I can't understand, after sinking into depression I made very few attempts during my sophomore year to improve my situation—until my therapist helped me create a plan. I simply accepted the fact that basketball made me miserable, and waited for it to end. Styron describes his state of mind as being one of "unfocused dread," which I can relate to. I was so immersed in my day-to-day anxiety that I couldn't think objectively about my situation. I was fixated on one thing—getting through the next practice or game.

7

"The depressed man realizes that all daily routines imply a belief in Tomorrow and are cruel jokes since of course tomorrow no longer exists."

- Tom Wolfe, *A Man in Full*

My worst symptoms occurred during games. Practices were bad enough, but games produced a special kind of dread. My performance on the court landed me out of the playing rotation and on the end of the bench with the walk-ons and injured players. But because I was on scholarship, the coaches didn't give up on me completely. When the outcome had been decided before a game ended, and I was sent in to play a few meaningless minutes, I hated being on the court with people watching me. I felt sure that my unreliable hands would produce something awful, like an airball from the free throw line, a humiliation for any player, even a 7-foot center whose primary job is to block shots and dunk. It's something beyond humiliation coming from a player who was recruited because of his shooting abilities.

So I sat on the bench, hoping that the score stayed too close for the coach to put me into the game. If our opponents were ahead, I pulled for us to get defensive stops and then score. Shamefully, when we had a lead I pulled for the other team to keep the score close. I sat there, desperately hoping not to play. When I stood up to cheer for teammates it was all an act. I didn't much care whether we won or lost. Losing was actually better, because at least there wouldn't be a celebration in the locker room, forcing me to pretend I was excited. When we won and my friends had played well, I felt jealous. When the game ended and I hadn't played, and we'd lost—which was how most games turned out—I breathed a sigh of relief.

I was so consumed with my secret goal of not playing that I didn't realize how bad my condition had become. I didn't have the mental capacity or fortitude to try to make a change. I look back on my behavior with shame.

Sometimes I lost myself in fantasies about being seriously injured in practice. If I'd had the choice to quit playing basketball forever—or, better yet, to see the sport banished from planet earth—I'd have been overjoyed. But quitting would mean losing my scholarship, and I couldn't justify putting financial pressure on my family to help me pay for the remainder of my schooling.

I felt trapped, because I wasn't sure I could endure two and a half more years of misery. Styron, a well-known and highly regarded American writer, explains: "Of the many dreadful manifestations of the disease, both physical and psychological, a sense of self-hatred—or, put less categorically, a failure of self-esteem—is one of the most universally experienced symptoms, and I had suffered more and more from a general feeling of worthlessness as the malady had progressed." I understand. I became altogether unconcerned with myself or my future and began indulging in shallow pleasures wherever I found them, with no regard for my own health or wellbeing. I used binge drinking and junk food eating as escapes. I also spent many empty hours mindlessly scrolling my phone.

8

I periodically spoke with family members in Oregon, who watched my games on the internet. They never saw my practices, so were under the illusion that I still had the skills they remembered from my high school days and my best freshman games at Regis. They wondered why I wasn't playing, and assumed the coach was treating me unfairly. Too ashamed to admit that I was no longer a good player, and that I didn't really want to play, I lied, and told everyone who cared that, yes, the coach was to blame, and that my poor performances during my brief on-court appearances were due to my not having time to establish a rhythm and work myself into the game. I said this so often that the dysfunctional part of my mind tried to believe it.

My dad urged me to politely ask the coach what I needed to do to earn more playing time. Those were moments when I had to face the truth: that I didn't want to play, and I didn't want to improve. What I wanted was to go unnoticed until the season ended. This made talking to the coach impossible. Instead of facing the truth, I lied to my dad, and to the rest of my family. Then I returned to the doublethink I'd been engaging in for months—believing my lie.

Coach served as my scapegoat. He lost his temper easily, and his style was not a good fit for my personality. But he wasn't the root cause of my problems, and he certainly wasn't the unapproachable tyrant that I made him out to be to my family. Had I gone to see him, he would have welcomed me into his office, listened patiently, and offered an honest response. But I knew I'd become a bad player, so why would I go ask for more playing time? It was clearly the correct decision to play other guards instead of me, and I was happy to remain on the bench.

Much of my anxiety and shame actually came from my projections of how my assistant coach, Eric Daniels, felt about me. He was an excellent coach and person, and gave me every opportunity to succeed. He had recruited me in Oregon, and he consistently stuck up for me at Regis. He encouraged me, and often checked with me to see how I was doing, but, unfortunately, his presence in the gym made me feel anxious and guilty for having let him down.

The graduate assistant, Steve Ledesma, seemed to intuitively understand what I was going through. He often ate lunch with me and spent time with me outside of basketball. I remember clearly how much his support meant to me, and I tried to offer similar support to struggling players when I became a graduate assistant, something that would be inappropriate coming from a head coach or a lead assistant.

I reached the lowest point in my depression at the University of Colorado Springs. While I watched from the bench, my teammates had an especially rough first half, after which Coach vehemently expressed his disappointment in our halftime meeting. After that, back on the court, my first halftime shot bounced off the backboard, and Coach saw it. All I remember is him screaming at me: "You don't want to play! You don't want to play!" So he'd seen through my pathetic secret, and now it had become public knowledge.

9

I was jealous of non-athlete friends who enjoyed a five week vacation between semesters, while I was stuck with my miserable sport twice per day. Scrolling social media, everyone I saw looked much happier than I was. We were given six days of freedom around Christmas, which were far from relaxing and rejuvenating. I tried to make time for everything and everyone, which made me feel like I hadn't made enough time for anything or anybody. The days raced by as I sacrificed sleep and crammed in as much as possible. I felt like an unhappy zoo animal that's released into the wild just enough to realize what it's been missing, but not long enough to enjoy its brief freedom.

Before I knew it my last day had arrived. I'd booked my flight back to Denver at the latest possible time—4:30am on the morning of our first practice back—foolishly thinking

I'd be able to enjoy my last evening in my hometown when I went out for pizza with my family and some close friends. Despite the warmth and love they gave me, I was overcome with dread and despair. With each passing moment my 3:15 am alarm was inching closer. After the alarm I could look forward to the hell of airport security, a crowded flight back to Denver, driving to campus, and showing up at the dreaded gym to resume my role as an underachieving disappointment. I hadn't even considered picking up a basketball during my days off, so I worried that my shot would feel worse than ever when I returned. I'd be a tired and nervous wreck all day.

So at dinner I faked smiles and did my best to joke with friends as I took sad bites of pizza even though I wasn't hungry. A heavy pressure rested in my chest. When my Oma told me she loved me as she was leaving I felt tears well up in my eyes, but I bit my lip and forced my emotions back down to where they came from. After dinner, when my friends headed happily to the bars, I headed home with only six hours of freedom left.

CHAPTER 8

SPORTS AND IDENTITY

1

A common (and dangerous) defense mechanism for struggling athletes is to pretend they no longer care about their sport. When I arrived at college there was no doubt in my mind that sports and the teams I played for mattered a lot. When I fell out of the playing rotation and became a failure in my own mind, my opinion changed. Suddenly basketball had no application to the real world—the world that actually mattered. Then, predictably, when my senior year began showing some hope that I might succeed, everything changed back. Basketball and my team became important again. Of course this was illogical. Basketball is either a waste of time or it isn't, and the question has nothing to do with how I happen to be doing on my team. There's a strong correlation between a player's attitude toward a team's goals and that player's standing on the team. Players unsatisfied with their role tend to blame the coaching staff and their system. In extreme cases they blame the sport, or even sports in general.

When I arrived at Regis there was an obvious divide on the team. The new players, coming from better team cultures, believed in playing hard and doing extra work after practice. Some of the players who had been on the team the year before, going 2-20 in conference play, made a point of showing everyone that they didn't really care about basketball. Sometimes they ridiculed teammates who were working to improve, and they were proud of showing up at practice hungover after a night of partying. They didn't hide their indifference after either wins or losses, and often mocked those who showed emotion. This defense mechanism became the cornerstone of the team and the program—yes, we suck, but who cares? We still get to party!

When I fell out of the rotation, I felt resentment. After watching a big win from the bench, I was jealous of the players who had contributed. I took every opportunity I could find to criticize the head coach and our team's record. I liked to joke about the small crowds that attended our games. As a defense mechanism for my damaged ego, I needed to make what I was failing at unimportant.

But my attempts at detachment from basketball contributed to my depression and anxiety. The worse I played, the harder I tried not to care, and the harder I tried not to care, the worse I played, and felt. This culminated in my therapist's diagnosis. Trying to believe that basketball didn't matter felt satisfying in the short term, but over time it made everything worse. Every day I spent hours doing what I tried to hate. The "flow states" that produce joyful experiences in sports require focused energy and commitment. Without meaningful engagement, time drags along, and misery accelerates. This happened to me at practice every day.

2

Even though I grew up with unconditional love from my family, my self-worth was based on athletic success. Sports gave me an identity, and became a sanctuary where I could hide from normal adolescent problems. I could feel successful thanks to my identity as a "jock."

Until I arrived at college, I'd never bothered to think about what I wanted to study, or what I might want to do with my life. My major college concerns were basketball, making friends, and meeting girls. I wanted the approval of my teammates, especially the upperclassmen, and I assimilated quickly and thoughtlessly to the team culture. One norm in the locker room was to joke and sometimes even brag about how many classes one had cut, and even to joke about how useless various classes were—like philosophy, chemistry, or history.

So, with little thought, I became a jock in college, just as I'd been one in high school. Academically, the generally accepted norm was to pick an easy major that would hopefully lead to adequate grades. I could drink on the weekends, play video games in my free time, and do just enough work to pass my classes.

I had vague dreams of playing professional basketball overseas after graduation, but as my freshman year played out, the foundation of the identity I'd built was shaken. In my sophomore year it came crashing down. My source of meaning and fulfillment became a source of agony instead.

3

"Sports are fine, but children must be exposed to other things by their mothers and fathers, and that includes books, reading, and learning."

- UCLA and Hall of Fame Coach John Wooden

In high school I was fairly good at "playing the game" academically. Sometimes I copied homework from friends and rarely paid close attention during classes. I was good at taking tests and could stay up late the night before to cram the material and end up knowing enough to perform moderately well. I sometimes cheated by paying serious students to give me encoded signs during a test, much like a third base coach gives signs to batters and base-runners. A subtle touch to the nose represented "A" on a Scantron test, and adjusting the bill of a cap represented "B". Without learning much of anything, I finished high school with a decent GPA. Most of my downtime from athletics was spent watching sports or playing video games. Aside from playing and following sports and hanging out with friends, nothing much interested me.

One positive side effect of my identity crisis was a sudden interest and commitment to academics. At the time I couldn't have articulated why I was suddenly committing so much energy toward my classes, but now it's clear what happened: I needed a new way to have control and to feel successful. The hard work and energy I'd devoted to basketball hadn't worked, and school offered a simpler path to success.

My academic performance improved, and earning good grades gave me a rare spike of positive emotion in the midst of a challenging year. When I did assigned reading, I found myself interested in the subjects being presented. Most surprisingly, I realized that paying attention and doing the work was far less stressful than missing classes, copying homework, and creating intricate systems to cheat on tests.

Math had always come naturally to me, so I signed up for Calculus I, and soon decided to major in mathematics. Surprisingly, solving math problems produced psychological relief. I actually looked forward to spending hours in the library alone with my math textbook. The experience taught me that focusing on something could be intrinsically pleasant. When I was hard at work on a math problem I wasn't worrying about my reputation on the team, or with the girls I liked who didn't like me back, or if I'd lose my scholarship. I earned As in most of my classes, which made me feel good.

4

For a while my transition to academics became an overcorrection. Finding some success in the classroom emboldened me to further ridicule the team, basketball, and sports in general. For a while, I even refused to watch sports on television. I fled the dumb jocks team and enlisted as a snobbish intellectual. I've seen other academically successful athletes trying to adopt the same view, pretending their sport was a chore that had to be endured as they worked toward their degrees.

But pretending not to care isn't really not caring. My snide remarks to teammates about how bad we were, and how pointless basketball was, were masks for my misery. The painful truth I wouldn't admit to myself was that I still wanted to contribute as a useful member of the team.

I still regard my high school baseball coach, Don Senestreo, as one of the best coaches I've ever played for. He used to tell us that there was a vulnerability in giving full effort, and that many of us, athletes and non-athletes alike, give less than full effort as a defense mechanism. It's only in looking back on my career that I really understand what he meant. When I encountered the most adversity in college, one of my responses was to stop trying to succeed. Subconsciously I knew that giving everything I had and continuing to fail would be a painful experience. What I didn't understand was that retreating from my problems, and protecting my ego, would be even more painful in the long term.

Coach Senestrero used to tell us that playing with full effort and engagement was the only guaranteed way to make the most of your time on the field and to avoid having any regrets. Now I understand.

I'll always regret my attitude and behavior during my sophomore year. Not only did my attempt to make basketball seem useless further diminish my mental health, it also detracted from my friends' experiences, some of them seniors trying to enjoy the last season they'd ever play.

CHAPTER 9

MENTAL TRAINING

1

While I outwardly pretended not to care anymore about basketball, I occasionally experienced waves of motivation to recover. I alternated between watching cliché-ridden self-help YouTube videos featuring overly exuberant life coaches, and binge drinking that I tried to believe made me rebellious.

The only training I had any familiarity with was physical training, so I hoped that pouring my effort into basketball workouts would produce confidence. Growing up, when I faced challenges I always fell back on my ability to grit my teeth and outwork everyone. Even if it meant spending four hours in the gym, or taking a thousand swings in the batting cages, I was determined to fix my problems with brute force.

But this attitude stopped working as I climbed the ranks of competition, and as a sophomore in college, it contributed to my mental spiral. Sometimes I went to the gym at 9:30 at night to put up shots alone, telling myself that this would be a heroic way out of my slump. I'd often been told that seeing the ball go through the net generates confidence. The trouble was, shooting alone in the gym, without pressure, was nothing remotely like shooting at practice in front of coaches and teammates, let alone in games. No amount of three-pointers made alone in the gym could cure me. I lived in a fog of confusion and hopelessness.

My therapist introduced a different approach for how to regain confidence and mental balance. She suggested that I should no longer think of anxiety as my enemy, and that instead of trying to get rid of it, trying to think or work my way out of it, I should in fact pay closer attention to it. To me this sounded impossible, even stupid, and I told her so as kindly as I could. But she persisted, claiming that my resistance to anxiety only made it worse. She explained that when anxiety arose, trying to fight it off made me worry more, increasing its intensity, something like a Chinese finger trap. She told me that paying attention to anxiety, and how it manifests physically, reduces its power.

As a way to practice this new approach to my mental issues, she introduced the practice of mindfulness meditation, and at the end of each therapy session she led me through a guided session. She had me sit upright in my chair with my eyes closed, and asked me to concentrate on my breathing. As I sat there, she periodically reminded me to pay attention to my breath. I was surprised to discover how difficult it is to focus on the breath without becoming distracted by thoughts.

After a few minutes of concentrating on breathing, she told me to visualize a situation that made me anxious. Shooting free throws was my choice. She told me to imagine what the court felt like under my feet, what it sounded like in the gym, how the ball felt in my hands, and what it was like to have my coach and teammates watching me. The goal was to re-create the anxiety that I felt in the actual situation. To my surprise, it worked. A similar, albeit less intense rush of tightness gripped my hands, chest, and face as I sat in her office thinking about free throws.

Next she had me focus directly on the sensations that my anxiety produced, without trying to change them or push them away. She claimed that this practice could help me respond more effectively to my anxiety, and also explained various frameworks that would prove the point. She told me to think of anxiety as something that would always be there with me on the court, and that instead of trying to get rid of it, I should practice simply noticing it, and refocusing my attention on the game.

At first this didn't strike me as a reasonable solution. The point of going to see her was to get rid of my mental anguish—I wanted to rid myself of anxiety and feel confident again. I wanted my hands to be relaxed, and my shot to feel the way it did in high school. Most of all, I wanted to be a contributing member of my team.

But I was desperate enough to take my therapist's advice. She recommended practicing ten minutes of meditation every day on my own. I did this sporadically at first, often skipping meditation for other supposedly more important things. But, even with irregular practice, I soon noticed that what I was doing worked. I improved at focusing attention on my breath for longer intervals, and was surprised to realize that when I didn't try to push the anxiety away, and instead focused on its sensations, their intensity was dramatically reduced.

2

The word "meditation" comes with unfortunate baggage. When my therapist first recommended it to me as a way of dealing with performance anxiety, the image that came to mind was one of wearing robes while listening to eastern flute music, sitting cross-legged, and chanting mantras. But deliberate mental training as I learned to practice it has nothing to do with clothing or music, and it transcends culture. Meditation in its simplest form is this:

1. With your eyes closed, sit relaxed and upright on a chair with both feet planted solidly on the ground.

2. Pay attention to the sensations of breathing. Focus your attention on the breath.

3. When you're distracted, bring your attention back to the breath.

4. Repeat step 3 again and again.

Some first-time meditators quickly realize how difficult this is. Others are thoroughly sidetracked by so many thoughts that they don't even recognize them as distractions. Something as simple as concentrating on breathing for 30 seconds without being distracted by thought can seem virtually impossible in the beginning—about as difficult as making five consecutive three-point shots would be for someone who'd never handled a basketball before. But, over time, the ability to focus on the breath improves, as surely as the ability to shoot a basketball improves with practice. Gradually, practitioners of meditation learn to maintain focus on the breath for increasingly longer intervals, and to notice distraction more quickly.

Eventually a meditator is able to broaden concentration to all sensations in the body, along with sounds, emotions (like anxiety), and even thoughts themselves. The objective is to become less reactive to these manifestations. Instead of being at the mercy of thought patterns, emotions, physical pain, and physical pleasure, the goal is to notice them clearly, and then respond to them knowingly and skillfully.

3

The meditation I practiced in the beginning was simple training in mindfulness of the breath. I tried to feel each inhalation and each exhalation. Counting the breaths as they came and went helped me stay centered. I tried to sit in a comfortable but firm posture, both feet firm on the floor, and pay close attention to the breath. Each time I noticed that my mind had run away (sometimes it took five minutes before I realized I was distracted) I brought my attention back to the breath.

Another form of mental training we practiced in her office was visualizing myself having success on the court. She asked me to perform three perfect jump shots in my mind—to feel myself balanced, extend into my shot, feel the ball come off my shooting hand cleanly, and then to watch the ball swish through the net. I was alarmed, and even frightened, at how I wasn't able to do this. Each time I tried to play the movie of a perfect jump shot in my mind, my mind habitually malfunctioned as soon as I made it to my release. Just as on the court, the ball always pulled off my left hand awkwardly. It was also hard to see the ball going through the net—the image of it clanking off the rim came to mind instead. This showed me, beyond doubt, that my problems on the court were primarily mental.

4

While people have been practicing meditation for thousands of years across diverse cultures and religions, it's only recently become widely accepted in Western culture. This popularity came about because here in the West we like to measure outcomes scientifically, and thanks to recent scientific advancements we've been able to track what actually happens to the brains and bodies of those who meditate. Accumulated evidence strongly suggests that the many anecdotal reports from meditators spanning millennia are quite likely valid.

I'm interested in the scientific research on how meditation and other kinds of mental training affect the brain, body and mind, but I also understand that much of the research currently being cited in books, apps, magazines and programs is either exaggerated, flawed, or fails to replicate.

In their helpful book *Altered Traits,* Dan Goleman and Richard Davidson do their best to outline the current state of the science, while distinguishing between good and bad evidence in support of the practice. They conclude that while much of the research in this space is flimsy at best, there's still enough solid evidence to suggest that the potential benefits of meditation are impressive.

Goleman and Davidson, after reviewing the research in its entirety, conclude that consistent meditators are, on average, less reactive to stress, better able to focus and concentrate, generally happier, have a greater pain tolerance, are more compassionate, and are less susceptible to mental health problems like anxiety and depression.

A consistent theme throughout *Altered Traits* is that inexperienced meditators enjoy such benefits while meditating, and immediately afterward, but that lasting, physical changes in the brain, and permanent positive changes in the mind, require consistent, long-term practice, which is also consistent with what yogis and meditation practitioners have been claiming for centuries. Short sessions of meditation for those who don't practice regularly yield short-term boosts in attention and cognitive ability, while long-term practitioners typically become sustainably more focused. The fact that even beginners enjoy benefits in concentration immediately after a session explains why I think pre-practice and pregame meditation can be such a helpful tool, even for those with no experience in the practice.

5

I had many teammates and coaches who drew mental strength and comfort from prayer and faith. I hope faithful athletes, coaches, parents and fans view the mental training I describe in this book not as contradictory to their current practices and beliefs, but rather complimentary. Meditation and visualisation can be done alongside prayer, and need not replace it. I'm not arguing in favor of one religion over another, but instead showing how simple mental exercises, if practiced consistently, can transform the mind of a young athlete who's trying to find peace and confidence.

6

I reluctantly started practicing, and it was messy at first. I tried for ten minutes each day, but it was hard to make myself sit in silence. When I sat down and closed my eyes I often felt uncomfortable, even frightened. Without my habitual distractions (my phone, TV, food, homework, conversations with friends, etc.), difficult thoughts and emotions often climbed to the surface of my mind. Rather than feeling calm and relaxed, I often felt distracted, sad, and frustrated. Maybe I can't do this either, I thought. Maybe I'm just broken beyond repair.

I tried, without much luck, to bring what I was practicing with me to the court. The intensity of my anxiety during practice was too much for my novice mindfulness to handle. Luckily, my therapist persisted. When I told her my anxiety hadn't subsided, she encouraged, even demanded, that I stick with it. Slowly, I began noticing small but important improvements.

CHAPTER 10

ADDING WOOD TO THE FIRE

1

While I struggled to work on my mind, my sophomore season dragged miserably along. I finished the year playing in 20 of our 27 games, averaging seven minutes per game. I averaged one point per game on 26% shooting from the field, and 21% from the three point line. The sound of the buzzer ending our final game came as a welcome relief.

Without basketball, I felt better about life again. My therapist and I came up with a plan. She insisted that a summer regimen of meditation, visualization, and scanning the body to pay attention to sensations would result in improved play the following season.

Back in southern Oregon, I felt more mature and grounded than I'd been the previous summer. I appreciated the small things in life that I'd paid no attention to during my months of depression—a hot cup of good coffee, or a conversation with a friend or family member.

So I enjoyed the summer, but with an oppressive darkness lingering in the back of my mind. On many nights I checked my phone for the date of the month just before going to bed, anticipating the end of my freedom and happiness in Oregon, where no one was tracking my performance, and I didn't have to see myself as a wasted scholarship. But August 20th would be here soon.

The mental training plan that my therapist had helped me set up consisted of daily meditation, visualization, and body scan practices totaling about 20 minutes per day. She gave me access to guided audio sessions from UCLA. I also practiced conjuring up images that made me anxious, and paying close attention to the feelings of anxiety without trying to push them away.

She'd encouraged me to use my time on the court to practice these components. Even though I believed that her suggestions could help me, I didn't give them enough time and effort. This is a common difficulty most of us have in trying to generate enough discipline to fully commit to a mental training practice. Even though I knew it had helped me in crucial ways at the end of my sophomore year, I didn't devote enough time to it in the summer. What I took more seriously were my basketball training, weight lifting, conditioning, and my leisure, probably because "mindfulness" is so difficult to define and evaluate. I couldn't be certain I was doing things correctly, and there was no clear way to measure progress. There were days when I ignored my mental training altogether.

2

My dad had always been deeply involved with my athletic career. I knew that coaching me and watching me compete was one of the great pleasures in his life. My subsequent struggles and unhappiness took an obvious toll on him. He was disturbed about my situation at Regis. Other loved ones must have been too when they streamed my weekend games, only to see me playing the last few meaningless minutes.

But I could tell that it affected my dad more than anyone else. One evening, he accompanied me to the gym to rebound for me during a summer shooting workout. In our workout I ran from spot to spot pumping in three-pointers, sometimes up to 20 in a row, and then went to the free throw line to knock down 10 straight.

While it was satisfying to perform that well in a workout, there was an elephant in the gym that, up until that evening, neither my dad nor I had ever acknowledged. I was sitting on a chair, dripping sweat, changing from my basketball shoes into sandals, when my dad sat down beside me. "Good shooting, kid," he said in his standard tone of playfulness and positivity.

"Thanks," I said, "hopefully I can save some for the season."

"You know, if you were somehow guaranteed to be calm, confident and relaxed during games next season, you really wouldn't have to touch a basketball again all summer." I looked up from my shoes and water bottle to meet his eyes. He looked tentative, and I knew he didn't want to hurt my feelings. I sat in silence and thought about what he'd said, and something shifted in me. I had to admit to myself that while pushing myself hard to improve my ball handling and shooting skills, I'd been ignoring the opportunity to improve my mental approach to the game, which was what needed improvement most.

While I'd obsessed over getting my three-point percentage in various drills to 70%, 75%, 80%; while I'd worried about shaving my mile time down in order to win the conditioning drills competition again; while I'd strained to add 20 pounds to my squats, dead-lifts, and clean-and-jerks, I'd been overlooking the fact that none of this would matter until I was able to rid myself of the crippling anxiety I'd carried through the previous season. And I realized my dad was right—if I somehow knew I could play free and remain calm and confident, shooting practice might remain important, but far less important than it seemed to me now. I knew how to shoot, but I couldn't shoot well during a minor anxiety attack. My physical training regimen was something of a fantasy world, a distraction from the uncomfortable area that needed improvement—my mind.

3

That day in the gym with my dad was when I truly made mental training a priority. For the rest of the summer I committed to meditation practice twice per day. I visualized my coach watching me shoot—glaring at me—and tried to manufacture other scenarios that had affected me. I was learning to recognize the anxiety and let it pass.

Beyond the mental reps that I did alone on the meditation chair during my offseason, I applied the practice to live situations. My most serious mistake during my sophomore year had been avoiding what frightened me. It's understandable for nervous and anxious people to try to avoid adversity, but it compounds the problem.

Yongey Mingyur Rinpoche is a Tibetan monk who spent much of his childhood studying and practicing meditation. By age 20 he'd already completed two three-year silent meditation retreats. He went on to become a renowned and beloved meditation teacher, something like the LeBron James of mindfulness. In his book *In Love with the World,* he describes his experience of leaving the comfort of his home, and the status and prestige of his role as a teacher, to embark on what's called a wandering retreat. In order to live the life of a homeless beggar, he left home in the middle of the night, leaving only a note for his loved ones. The purpose of his retreat was to test and refine the mental skills he'd been honing his entire life. Yes, his mind was relaxed at his monastery, but would it remain balanced when he slept on the streets, or when he was forced to beg for food in order to survive? He writes the following:

"Tibetans have an expression for deliberately increasing the challenges of maintaining a steady mind: adding wood to the fire. Generally, people go through life taking note of those experiences that recurrently enflame our anger or anxiety or fear—and then we try to avoid them, telling ourselves things like, *I can't watch scary movies. I cannot be in big crowds. I have a terrible fear of heights, or of flying, or of dogs, or the dark.* But the causes that provoke these responses do not go away; and when we find ourselves in these situations, our reactions overwhelm us. Using our inner resources to work with these issues is our only true protection, because external circumstances change all the time and are therefore not reliable."

4

My therapist didn't define the method that helped me overcome my fears, but when I researched the subject I understood that she was using "exposure therapy" as defined by the American Psychological Association:

"Exposure therapy is a psychological treatment that was developed to help people confront their fears.

When people are fearful of something, they tend to avoid the feared objects, activities, or situations. Although this avoidance might help reduce feelings of fear in the short term, over the long term it can make the fear become even worse. In such situations, a psychologist might recommend a program of exposure therapy in order to help break the pattern of avoidance and fear. In this form of therapy, psychologists create a safe environment to 'expose' individuals to the things they fear and avoid. The exposure to the feared objects, activities, or situations in a safe environment helps reduce fear and decrease avoidance."

I'd done all the fear avoidance I could manage in my sophomore season. When I went to the gym to shoot on my own, it was always when the coaches wouldn't be there. In practices I tried to hide from the ball whenever I could, and tried especially to avoid shooting free throws.

I hated feeling sad, lonely, or embarrassed, and tried to compensate for these feelings with junk food, mindless television, and alcohol. Finally, meditation forced me to confront negative emotions, to face them instead of hiding from them.

If you suffer from anxiety you have two options—you can try to make your world safer, or try to make yourself stronger. There's plenty of adversity in athletics and life, so the latter makes more sense. The problem you're trying to avoid will show up someday, somewhere, no matter what you do. Seeking it out is better than shrinking from it. With

gradual exposure to fearful experiences, athletes can reduce their fears and respond to them successfully.

I searched out opportunities to practice what I'd been
trying to learn in meditation and visualisation. My comfort zone was shooting alone in the gym or with my Dad
or Opa rebounding, and I'd been avoiding playing pick-up
ball with my old high school teammates and friends, because I didn't want them to see how far I'd fallen from my
high school days. Playing with them wouldn't produce the
level of gloom I'd experienced back in Denver, but it would
serve as an opportunity to get useful mental reps in.

When I walked into the gym and saw my friends, familiar pressure and tightness built in my chest, hands and
face. Instead of trying to push the anxiety away, I shifted attention to the physical sensations it produced. This
helped, until I became distracted. As I played, I repeated
the process over and over, all summer long, and I gradually
improved. Rinpoche again: "Adding wood to the fire deliberately brings difficult situations to the forefront so that we
can work with them directly. We take the very behaviors or
circumstances that we think of as problems and turn them
into allies."

5

A few weeks before returning to Regis as a junior, I went
with my family to Laguna Beach, where continuous
pick-up games were played on outdoor basketball courts
throughout the day. It was a good opportunity to get some
cardio in on vacation, so I took my tennis shoes to the
beach and stood waiting to be picked for a team. Players

were sweating under a hot California sun, and the vibe on the court was competitive, because a losing team had to wait at least 20 minutes to get another chance.

When I finally got picked to play I felt the familiar anxiety and fear and started the game tentatively. Before long I realized that many of my teammates were football players, and that I had more basketball talent than any of them. If we wanted to win I had to score. My teammates fed me the ball repeatedly, and I came off screens aggressively and slashed to the basket scoring layups over defenders. I took semi-contested threes without hesitation. I barked out instructions for my teammates and worked hard on defense.

On the final play I made an aggressive side dribble move and knocked down a fade-away three, giving us the win. I high-fived my teammates and then sat courtside waiting for our next match-up.

This was the best I'd felt on a basketball court in years. In Laguna Beach nobody knew who I was, and I could reinvent myself, and my shot came cleanly off my shooting hand without effort.

6

As athletes we color our experiences with stories about how things are going—stories inspired by our current stature on a team, our statistics, and our opinions about how things *should* be going. We continually evaluate ourselves both individually and as team players, and then compare our evaluation to our expectations.

We can't completely rid ourselves of these stories, and we shouldn't try to. A season inevitably consists of pains and struggles, wins and losses, good and bad individual performances, and the long journey offers a meaningful context for each game. But a preoccupation with personal stories can easily become counterproductive. If an athlete identifies with the stories she's telling herself, she risks getting trapped by them, making it all but impossible to connect with the present moment.

Looking back at my sophomore season, I remember showing up for practices and games as if wrapped in a wet blanket of negative stories. I often tried to promise myself that today I'd play with confidence and somehow recapture what I'd felt in previous years. But I always reverted to anxiety, too much self-concern, and tentative play.

By mid-season I was trapped. Shooting about 20% from the three-point-line and 50% from the free throw line in both practice and games, I reasoned that even if I somehow had a good game, it wouldn't save my season or improve my situation much. So, each day, my "story" negatively affected my effort, attitude, and confidence.

In high school I'd been just as wrapped up in these stories, and they'd made me feel good about myself. I'd had no way of knowing that my pride and addiction to status would be my undoing when times got tough. I've since learned that focusing on the present moment is the only way out of this trap. Trying to treat every workout, practice, and game as if it were the first and last one I'd ever play changed everything.

Meditation is the practice of continually dropping the stories we tell about ourselves about our own lives and identities, and reconnecting, again and again, to the present moment.

Chapter 11

BABY STEPS

1

Back home from Laguna Beach, I was surprised to find an email from my therapist asking me to call her. She told me she'd taken a new job in Florida, which meant we could no longer work together in the coming year. She also told me how confident she was that I was on the right track, and encouraged me to keep practicing what we'd been working on, and to find someone else at Regis.

I thanked her for all she'd done for me, but when I hung up the phone I felt raw and afraid. All summer I'd pictured myself having her support in the upcoming season. Her office had become a sanctuary where I could speak to someone who really seemed to understand what I was dealing with. But I was determined to keep practicing.

2

I didn't go back to Denver with high expectations. I'd started off my first two seasons with ambitious goals, but this year my modest hope was to avoid misery, and to recover at least some of my skills on the court. In my first moments in the gym with the newly formed team, I felt the familiar rush of anxiety, but I was determined not to let it overcome me.

Now I had a modest toolkit for dealing with anxiety, and it worked at our first practice. To end every practice Coach lined the team up on the baseline and then tossed the ball down the court. We all had to run after the ball and stop it before it reached the free throw line, sometimes saving it by tipping it back to other teammates. Whoever ended up with the ball had a chance to end practice immediately by knocking down two straight free throws. Missing a free throw meant we lined up to repeat the process, until someone made the free throws. I'd always avoided the ball as if it was a live hand grenade.

Here, though, was a chance to make a real change, to prove something to myself. In that first junior season practice I sprinted after the ball ahead of my teammates and grabbed it with both hands. Approaching the free throw line, I felt every eye in the gym on me. Thoughts of air balling or badly bricking the shot flashed through my mind. As I stepped up I shifted focus to my feet on the floor. Even though I'd been practicing for this all summer, I felt tense when I released the ball. It bounced softly on the front rim, hit the backboard, then dropped through the net. My second shot felt good coming out of my hands. It floated toward the hoop, rattled around and popped out—an in-and-out miss. As I walked to the baseline I took some deep breaths and gathered myself. I was glad I'd voluntarily put myself in that position, and I wanted more of that feeling. The next day after practice I sprinted for the ball again, and, though nervous, knocked down both free throws. This small event was a major turning point in my college career.

When we think about courage in the context of athletics, we usually mean heroic feats of grace under pressure—Michael Jordan's game winning shot in the NBA Finals, or a walk-off World Series home run by Derek Jeter. These accomplishments rightly come with a shower of praise. In contrast, sinking two free throws after practice is so pathetically ordinary that it's embarrassing to admit what it meant to me at the time. But, for me, it was one short step in the right direction. And until I began making those steps, I'd been hopelessly mired in a bad place. We have to give ourselves credit for small improvements, otherwise we'd likely stay stuck forever.

3

On an off day during the preseason a group of us organized a halfcourt pickup game of three on three. The teams were evenly matched and competition was intense. On game point, when my man drove hard with his left hand and I sprinted to cut him off, he jump-stopped in the paint, and as he moved into his shot I stripped him cleanly. He called a foul, and I protested mildly before giving in and letting them have the ball back. Then he finished the game with a mid-range jumper and celebrated.

I was sitting on the baseline to catch my breath before the next game and Dylan, my best friend on the team, sat next to me and said, "You've got to stop taking that kind of shit. That was a clean strip."

"I know it was," I said.

"Then why'd you let him take the ball back?"

I just sat there looking down at the floor.

I've always gone out of my way to please people, because any kind of conflict stresses me out. I get along well with almost everyone, and it wasn't until that specific day in my life that I understood that this isn't always a good thing. Part of my troubles as a player, and a person, stemmed from my desire to please people around me at the cost of being myself. I desperately wanted my coaches to like me, and I was shy and timid around them, both on the court and off. I wanted my teammates to like me, which led me to party every weekend even though I didn't really want to. I wanted girls to like me, but girls don't usually like guys without a spine.

During my junior year I started to tap into my dark side in a healthy way. When Coach yelled at me, instead of reflexively feeling bad about myself, I decided whether his criticism was fair, and if it wasn't I politely ignored him. I also became more assertive on the court by voicing my opinion instead of saying whatever I thought people wanted to hear. The change made me feel more integrated as both a player and a person.

4

During my junior season my mental training began to show itself on the court. There were clear examples of tangible improvement (and one form of consequential confusion, which I'll get to later). Through my freshman and sophomore years, seeing my head coach come out of his office above the gym threw me into a minor panic. Now when I saw him, feelings of anxiety arose, but instead of trying to fight them off I simply paid attention to them, and then let them subside. Mistakes on the court that brought scorn from my coach became less important.

I played sparingly off the bench in our first few games, still feeling nervous, but I wasn't overwhelmed with self-doubt. In our fourth game of the year I made my first couple of shots off the bench, and felt a level of confidence that I hadn't experienced since high school. I ended up making six of nine shot attempts and scoring 17 points.

But the team had a poor season. We got blown out of many games, and I bounced in and out of the rotation. It was another battle, with one important difference—I wasn't miserable anymore. If I'd played well, and enjoyed success, the shift in my mental life might have been attributed to external circumstances. But in almost every way my junior year was as bad as the prior year had been. I was yelled at by my coach, I sometimes underperformed, and we repeatedly, as the saying goes, got our asses kicked. I dealt with bouts of anxiety and depression but knew I was stronger and had effective tools to deal with negative experiences. I didn't waste time worrying about the next practice or game. I enjoyed my free time and my classes. I preferred being awake to being asleep. No longer plagued by anxiety, I made 79% of my free throws. I wanted to play and wanted to win, and wanted my friends on the court to play well. While my roommate Brian and I bonded over our shared miseries during the season, we also enjoyed life.

But clear proof of the fact that I wasn't yet connecting with sports in a truly meaningful way was the countdown calendar Brian and I kept on our wall, checking off each day as we wished the season away.

5

I had a few appointments with the newly hired sports psychologist on campus. I liked him enough, but our chemistry was nothing like I'd had with my old therapist. She was wise and inspiring, he seemed like he was relaying concepts he'd memorized out of a textbook. So after a few meetings I stopped going, and thankfully, my mind continued to improve.

6

"Breaking addiction is socially unacceptable."

- Naval Ravikant

On a Saturday night my roommate/teammate and I drove to the pre-game, where most of our team would drink together before heading out to larger parties. When we arrived, the video game console was set up for our traditional beginning: four players at a time played Mario Kart, racing against each other. Each competitor had a full beer on hand, and the beer had to be downed before the race was finished. In order to drink the controller had to be set down on the floor. Innovative strategies evolved based on the map being raced and the competition. For example, when launched off a power ramp no control was necessary, so that was the time to take huge swallows of beer. Players capable of it started races by chugging full beers so they could then race without any breaks in momentum. The winner kept his controller, and the three losers gave theirs up to new players. Other competitions followed Mario racing: King's Cup, Beer Pong, and Flip Cup, all accompanied with constant banter, trash talking, and dancing and laughter. By the time we left for larger parties everybody was at least half hammered, stumbling through a cold Denver night. The next morning I often woke up with a headache and upset stomach.

This was the standard routine every weekend for as long as I'd been at Regis. As my junior year unfolded, I knew that drinking too much every weekend was senseless. After a productive week of training, meditation, and math homework, getting drunk felt something like shaking an etch-a-sketch to obliterate everything I'd created. But I felt a close connection with my best friends, and going to pre-games became an obligation for the sake of preserving my friendships. Some nights I secretly filled my empty beer can with water.

CHAPTER 12

CATCHING UP TO THE CAR

1

Before my third season at Regis, our head coach decided that, after 38 years, this would be his last as a coach. On February 6th, 2015, Regis hosted Colorado Christian, and celebrated his career. Our gym that always held small crowds was transformed into a raucous environment. Former players from various decades and their families packed the house. Even NBA star Chauncey Billups was in attendance (Coach Porter and Billups co-founded the Porter Billups Leadership Academy, which provides academic and leadership training to at-risk inner city students in the Denver area.)

Colorado Christian was heavily favored, but, propelled by the energy of the crowd, we somehow stayed close, finally losing by three points in a game that was exciting from start to finish. At game's end Coach Porter got a standing ovation. In the locker room he was emotional, and thanked us for the effort we gave on his big night. I felt my resentment for him melt away. Despite his shortcomings as a coach late in his career, I have respect for him as a man. He instilled values in us that transcend basketball, and even in our most contentious moments on the court I knew that he loved and cared about me as a person. Coach Porter kept me on scholarship despite my poor performance, which he didn't have to do. I'm forever grateful for what he gave me.

For years I'd used the dysfunction of our team and my criticisms of my coach as excuses for my basketball problems. These excuses implied that with a new coach my problems would be solved. Now I felt something like the dog that finally catches up to the car. What if I didn't improve? I felt vulnerable without my built-in excuses.

2

At season's end we had no coach to report to and assumed that the hiring process would last until we left for the summer. We stopped playing and working out, and our weekend dissipation increased. Some teammates dropped into the risky routine of smoking weed whenever possible, and then having to worry about a random drug test.

But not long after our lives of relative leisure began, the athletic department announced that the field of those who had applied for the Regis coaching job had been narrowed to two, and that we'd meet the finalists in the locker room.

When Brady Bergeson addressed us, he carried an aura of intensity into the room. Before he spoke to us he carefully printed two words on the whiteboard, and underlined them: <u>RMAC CHAMPIONSHIP</u>. The first thing he said to us was, "This is going to happen here under my watch. It might take one year, it might take five years, but this is going to happen." Having been at or near the bottom of the conference for nearly a decade, the thought of an RMAC Championship seemed impossible to us.

After guaranteeing a championship, he passed out slips of paper and pens and asked us to list the three hardest workers on the team, and the three best teammates. After we handed in our slips of paper he introduced himself and outlined his coaching philosophy. By the time the meeting ended we all knew who our new coach would be.

Coach Bergeson arrived on campus with two weeks of eligible practice time left before we'd take our finals and leave for the summer. In our first meeting he told us that in those two weeks we'd learn about each other, and he'd decide who would remain on the team. I had good reason to be worried. The team hadn't made the conference play-offs during my three years, and my stats had been terrible. I couldn't imagine a reason why a new coach wouldn't want to start fresh and recruit his own players.

His intensity was something none of us were used to, and a barrage of negative thoughts consumed me. What would I do if he cut me from the team? I was a year away from graduating with a degree in mathematics, with no student debt. I had no idea how many of my Regis credits would transfer to another school. After three lackluster years of basketball at Regis, I had little if any chance of winning a scholarship anywhere else.

3

Our autonomic nervous system is subdivided into the sympathetic and parasympathetic nervous systems. Our nervous systems activate automatically as a response to incoming stimuli. Our sympathetic nervous systems activate to generate energy for a fight, flight, or freeze response to a perceived threat. Many changes occur in the body with sympathetic activation—our pupils dilate, our digestive tracts shut down, our heart rates climb, blood rushes to our extremities, and we fixate on the perceived threat.

This response was selected through evolution, and it served our species well. When our ancestors were foraging for food and they came across a lion or a tiger, those with a powerful response were more likely to survive the encounter. This is a very useful response when someone jumps out of a dark alley toward you with a knife. But being in fight, flight, or freeze mode is destructive when you're trying to make a clutch free throw or having a conversation with a cute girl. In these instances, we want our parasympathetic nervous system, the system that activates when we're in a relaxed and composed state, to be activated.

Between every stimulus and response there's always a space. As you train through meditation, that space grows wider, and wider, giving the meditator a greater opportunity to respond skillfully to the incoming stimuli. As I practiced meditation and mindfulness, I found myself able to respond, rather than react, to my experiences in skillful ways. An especially clear example of my improved mind came during my first tryout with the new coach.

Our first tryout session consisted of cutthroat half-court games of three versus three. All potentially returning players knew what was at stake, and we played harder than we had since early the previous season. In one of the first few possessions, I ran hard and fast off a solid pin-down in the corner, took a pass from the top of the key near the free throw line with plenty of space to shoot, rose up, and nervously aimed the ball at the basket. In what felt like slow motion, I watched the ball fall pathetically short of the rim and brush the net below it—a shameful airball—and the first shot Coach Bergeson had ever seen me take.

The familiar rush of embarrassed anxiety hit my chest and hands, while my flushed face turned hot—a sympathetic nervous system response, I was in fight, flight, or freeze mode. Ordinarily this would have led to a mental collapse. Cortisol, the stress hormone, would have flooded my brain; I'd be terrified of another awful shot and more embarrassment; I'd do my best to hide from the ball by pump faking and passing instead of shooting.

But this time as anxiety hit me, I felt my attention shift to the sensations of my feet on the floor and the feeling of my breath, just as I'd practiced it thousands of times while meditating. I let the feelings wash over me, and I redirected my attention to the present moment. I understood that the sensations in my face, chest, and hands had nothing to do with *me* or *who I am*. Usually after an airball I'd try to protect my fragile ego with the charade of looking at my hands and then wiping them on my jersey, to suggest that the ball had slipped. I might have even yelled "Fuck!" as an indication that something out of the ordinary had ruined the shot. Or I might have laughed and tried to look bewildered.

This time I said, "Nice screen" to the teammate who'd freed me up for the shot, found my spot on defense, took some deep belly breaths, and turned my attention to the next play. Recognizing my physical sensations for what they were not only destabilized their power over me, but also allowed my negative thoughts to subside. My parasympathetic nervous system kicked back in.

I remember this moment so vividly because it surprised me. I could scarcely believe how I'd handled it by doing exactly what I'd taught myself to do. I felt empowered. Later in the same scrimmage I caught fire from the three point line, and I remained calm and composed with success, just as I had with failure. Instead of showing pride after sinking a shot, I shifted my attention to the next play, sometimes after complimenting the passer or screener who'd helped me find space to shoot. I finished the scrimmage satisfied that I'd made a good first impression.

4

After the scrimmage we went to the weight room expecting to stretch and maybe do some core strength exercises to end the day. Instead, Coach set up a weightlifting circuit where we competed against each other. The workout consisted of lunges while holding weights overhead, then burpees, and finally pull-ups.

Halfway through it all of us were suffering beyond anything we'd ever experienced at Regis. With each burpee I threw myself onto the floor, raised my chest and used my quivering arms to push to my knees, then stood and jumped an inch or two off the floor and clapped my hands overhead. Nobody could do more than one pull-up at a time. I panted for breath, my muscles burned, and my teeth hurt.

I knew this was a test to see who might quit, and I was determined to finish it, even if I ended up in the hospital. After my final overhead lunge I collapsed to the floor in pain. Besides the pain, I felt gratitude and joy that the workout was over. When I regained a sense of time and place, a wave of nausea hit me. I crawled to the trash can just in time to vomit over the rim. After my stomach emptied I fell back to the floor and saw that most of my teammates, looking wretched, were still struggling to finish. Then I was yelled at by Coach for not cheering them on.

I'd entered a brand new sporting world.

5

After that first day three players informed Coach that they wouldn't be coming back. My roommate was one of the players who quit. He'd grown to hate basketball during his time at Regis and wanted to enjoy what was left of his college experience without the burden of athletics. I tried not to envy him, and was sad to see him go.

For the rest of the week things didn't let up much. We competed intensely on the court, followed by brutal workouts in the weight room. Over the weekend something unusual happened—none of us went to parties or drank alcohol. We were physically and mentally drained, and competing for roster positions and scholarships.

Our last practice came on a Thursday morning, and my meeting with Coach was scheduled for the afternoon. Even though I thought I'd played well during the tryout, I was an unathletic "shooter" with three seasons of subpar statistics, so I was worried that I'd be cut from the team.

When I walked into Coach's office I was light-headed, so nervous I could barely speak. He began by telling me that I'd done well in the hardest-working and best teammate ratings from my teammates. He appreciated that during the weight room competitions and on the court I'd pushed myself to the point of exhaustion.

I attribute some of my ability to withstand the pain to my meditation practice. Rather than reacting to the intense feelings of pain and exhaustion, I remember noticing them, just as I'd practiced again and again on the meditation chair. I also noticed the impulse to shut down, and often ignored it, knowing that I'd be rewarded for my willingness to push through.

Coach went on to acknowledge my deficiencies as a player, and said he had confidence that I could find my shooting touch again, but my slow feet and lack of athleticism wouldn't likely be a good fit in his defensive system. Finally, he said that he'd be happy to keep me on scholarship if I promised to show up and be a good teammate every day, even if I didn't get much playing time as a senior. He also told me I'd have a fair shot to earn a spot in the rotation if I improved in various areas. I was happy to agree.

Then Coach told me that during his first two weeks on campus he'd met professors who mentioned having me in class and told him I was a serious student. Because of my academic success in the previous two years I was eligible for a substantial academic scholarship as a senior, allowing Coach to cut my athletic scholarship almost in half and use the savings on new recruits. That must have influenced his decision to keep me around. My commitment to academics had paid off in a huge way.

CHAPTER 13

THE INNER GAME

1

My relief at remaining on the team didn't have much to do with basketball. I was happy about graduating with a math degree and without student loans to worry about. Even though I was committed to bringing a good attitude to my senior season, I had little hope I'd earn significant playing time.

I'd already begun thinking about life after basketball, which was why I accepted an internship to work for International Children's Network in Peru for the first half of the summer. One of my duties there was helping set up sponsorships for impoverished children so that their basic needs, like warm clothing and school supplies, could be met. I also tutored children after school in math, writing, and English. The extreme poverty I witnessed was shocking and depressing: beautiful children and their families crammed together in concrete caves, some of the parents reeking of alcohol. I connected with many Peruvian children who endured far more adversity than I'd ever faced, and I felt uncomfortable for having been consumed with problems that didn't seem to matter much anymore. Seeing poor children manage to laugh, smile, and push forward despite their sorry circumstances put my own troubles into a clearer perspective, and I hope my work there helped them as much as it did me.

In my free time I became a tourist, backpacking into Colca Canyon and visiting Machu Picchu. It became the longest period of time since elementary school that I'd gone without playing basketball.

2

Even though I'd almost given up hope of making the playing rotation, my extended break from basketball bothered me. I worried that my shot and ball-handling skills would suffer, and that the skill gap between my teammates and me would be wider than ever.

Then I was surprised to find how helpful the extended break turned out to be. Ever since I was six years old I'd been immersed in sports, always trying to improve. Sure, sometimes I'd take a few days off to go camping in the summer, but even then the pressure to improve was always on my mind. Six weeks off from basketball gave me a healthy distance from the sport and allowed me to think about it more clearly.

Chivay, Peru is a small town 12,000 feet above sea level. In my living quarters there was no connection to the internet, which proved to be a blessing. Without the opportunity to train in basketball, or hang out with friends, or go to parties, or scroll my phone, I found space to reflect on my athletic career and my life. For the first time in years there were periods of time with nothing to do and no one to impress or report to.

Before my identity shift as a sophomore I'd rarely read the assigned reading in my classes, or read anything worthwhile during my free time. I'd begun reading meaningful books as a junior, and in Peru the obvious truth finally became clear: there are people who know a lot more about life than most of us do, and for centuries they've been including their wisdom in books. I had plenty of time to read in Peru, and had brought books with me that would prove to be transformative.

I also spent time writing in a journal. Soon after I started writing, it became clear to me that what I truly wanted was to feel like part of the team, and enjoy playing basketball again. I wanted to earn a spot in the rotation and play meaningful minutes in every game. When I accepted this, I started figuring out what I had to do to make it happen. I mapped out a training program for the rest of the summer. Up until then my goals had always been vague, like wanting to "play better" or "feel better." Now I had something clearly defined to aim at.

3

One of the sports books I had with me was *The Inner Game of Tennis* by Tim Gallwey, a tennis pro who became a trainer. He described many of my hang-ups on the basketball court with surprising clarity. He makes a distinction between "Self 1" and "Self 2". Self 1, the ego mind, is the part of us that's wrapped up in expectations, fears, worries, and stories about ourselves. Self 2 is the part of us that's intrinsically skilled, quiet, and confident. Self 1 is the thinking mind, Self 2 is the doing or "being" mind.

He explains that for most of his playing career Self 1 dominated Self 2, and that the same was true for most of his students. As his training philosophy evolved, he began giving fewer directives to students, finding that explicit instructions about form and technique often influenced the players' thinking minds, and ultimately got in the way. When he told the players to pay attention to their bodies on the court, and simply let their bodies hit the ball, their strokes improved dramatically.

His message made sense to me. Reflecting on my own athletic career, I remembered that my best performances came when I wasn't thinking about what to do next. I was relaxed and spontaneous, and trusted that I'd know how to react when the moment came. My best shooting happened when I'd forgotten all about my form, and my hottest hitting streaks in baseball came when I forgot about my swing. I played my best when I wasn't consciously trying to.

He argues convincingly that the secret to achieving these flow states is not by trying harder to play well, but by developing focus, concentration, and non-judgmental awareness. This is how an athlete trains in "the inner game."

4

In American culture, and specifically American athletic culture, we're trained to label things as being either good or bad, and to chase after the good and stomp out the bad. As I grew up I wore my self-criticism as a badge of honor. I thought that my athletic success was mostly due to my refusal to accept failure and then fight my way to success.

When I didn't play well I'd clap my hands together hard and say to myself and anybody listening something like, "I can't make a fucking shot!" When I played well my ego swelled, and I wanted everybody in the gym to know how good I was. Like many athletes, sometimes I hid my insecurities under a blanket of false confidence and self-praise.

Gallwey writes: "The first skill to learn is the art of letting go the human inclination to judge ourselves and our performance as either good or bad. Letting go of the judging process is a basic key to the Inner Game... When we unlearn how to be judgmental, it is possible to achieve spontaneous, focused play."

As I thought about his advice under the blankets in my chilly Peruvian hostel, I realized that somewhere underneath my self-criticism and pride was the quiet, sustainable confidence he describes. When I shot three-pointers alone in the gym, sometimes Self 2 emerged, and I could sink shots at a high percentage from all over the court. I moved from spot to spot with fluidity and ease, letting my body shoot.

But when the bright lights came on and I was competing for playing time in front of coaches, Self 1 took over, trying to control my play, afraid of making mistakes, and desperate to do well. When I missed a shot I was furious, and when I made one I was proud.

I thought about what it would be like to feel like I did alone in the gym in the face of pressure and competition.

5

As a player and coach, Phil Jackson won a total of 13 NBA titles, more than anyone else in history. He earned the nickname "Zen Master" for his uncommon approach to coaching inspired by Zen Buddhism. Instead of standing up and screaming at his players and the referees during games, Jackson usually sat quietly on the bench, as if he were a casual observer.

Instead of calling timeouts to break an opposing team's momentum, he often let his players suffer a negative run while encouraging them to stay composed. His offensive system was much more team-oriented than the isolation styles popular in the league. And he trained his players mentally to protect them from the problems he'd faced as a player. In *Sacred Hoops*, he writes:

"When I was a player, not surprisingly, my biggest obstacle was my hypercritical mind. I'd been trained by my Pentecostal parents to stand guard over my thoughts, meticulously sorting out the 'pure' from the 'impure.' That kind of intense judgmental thinking—this is good, that's bad—is not unlike the mental process most professional athletes go through every day. Everything they've done since junior high school has been dissected, analyzed, measured, and thrown back in their faces by their coaches, and, in many cases, the media. By the time they reach the pros, the inner critic rules."

A hyper-judgmental attitude is pervasive in sports, and I'd become one of the countless confused athletes who mistakenly viewed my judgmental mind as a virtue. Jackson encountered many coaches who adopted this spirit into their philosophies. They created rating systems that reached far deeper than conventional statistics, evaluating "good" or "bad" actions on the court and posting players' scores in the locker room as a way of incentivizing "good" actions. He writes:

"That approach would have been disastrous for a hypercritical player like me. That's why I don't use it. Instead, we show players how to quiet the judging mind and focus on what needs to be done at any given moment. There are several ways we do that. One is by teaching the players meditation so they can experience stillness of mind in a low-pressure setting off the court."

6

Back in Oregon I felt enthusiastic about basketball. The first time I walked into a gym I experienced a deep appreciation for the beauty and sounds of the court. Even the simple rhythm of dribbling a ball was exciting.

And my shot felt unusually smooth and rhythmic. The slight glitch that I'd been struggling with since my senior year of high school was somehow gone. The extended break had resulted in a necessary reset. It led me to believe that occasional time off from a sport can do an athlete more good than harm. Backpacking, experiencing a new culture, joining a meditation retreat, any of these can result in an understanding that might never occur to an athlete obsessed with incessant work and improvement.

I had eight weeks before returning to Regis. During previous summers I'd felt that the momentum of my training had often been interrupted. I love family camping trips, but I told my parents that Monday through Friday I'd need to stay home so I could train. In the past my training had also been stalled by the occasional night out with friends, when I'd eventually find myself drunk at two in the morning, and my only goal the next day was getting rid of an awful headache. So I let my friends know that I wouldn't be quite the same friend I'd been in previous years.

Maintaining those boundaries wasn't easy, but it resulted in eight weeks of uninterrupted progress.

7

Phil Jackson hired George Mumford to teach his players about meditation and how it relates to sports, and in Peru I read Mumford's book, *The Mindful Athlete*. Jackson credits Mumford for being a critical asset during the Bulls and Lakers dynasties. He introduced mindfulness practices to Kobe Bryant, who became committed to meditation throughout his playing career.

In his book, Mumford explains the Buddha's teachings about "right effort" and "wrong effort" as they relate to athletic improvement, beginning with an example from Greek mythology. In the Myth of Sisyphus, Sisyphus' wrongdoings have landed him in an eternal hell, endlessly pushing a huge boulder up a steep mountainside. Every effort fails, and the boulder rolls back down the mountain, so Sisyphus has to begin again, and again, and again.

Mumford writes: "The Myth of Sisyphus has been interpreted in many ways, but for our purposes let's just assume that Sisyphus is exerting 'wrong effort.' He represents that part of our nature that's conditioned to believe that life is a grind and that to 'win,' we have to fight our way to the top, focus on the destination rather than the journey, and swim hard upstream against the current even if that current loops us back through the same unending cycle of stress.

"Sisyphus lives in the land of extremes. In mainstream sports, this is essentially the familiar archetype of the forceful gladiator who must crush the opponent and win at all costs in an us-against-them world of high-stakes combat.

Anger and/or fear are what motivate action. There has to be either victory or failure, triumph or defeat."

During my many hours in the gym at 8:30 p.m. as a desperate sophomore, getting shots up alone, dreading the upcoming 5 a.m. practice, I was Sisyphus in hell. I'd been persuaded by the "Ball is Life" crowd that in order to become and remain a great shooter you have to get in 1,000 shots per day. Training has to be a struggle, something to fight and wrestle with. Supposedly, great shooters are often in the gym at 1 a.m. while everyone else is asleep. Stories about Kobe Bryant waking up his trainer to go to the gym in the middle of the night are well known among basketball people.

But finally I came to understand that my attitude toward my training was proof that I didn't think I was good enough. There was a false hope that if I just trained hard enough, and outworked everyone around me, my reward in the end would be peace and confidence. Then I realized that to cultivate sustainable confidence and mental balance, you have to practice it in the present moment. Yes, sometimes you have to push through pain, discomfort, and exhaustion, but training in athletics doesn't have to be an unending and miserable struggle.

8

My eight weeks of training before returning to campus were much different than other years had been. Persuaded by Mumford, I adopted the mindset that three reps at game speed with clear focus and intention did more good than 100 reps with a clouded and distracted mind. My workouts became shorter and more intense, and less stressful.

When I focused hard on my mental training, beginning and ending each day with 20 minutes of meditation and visualization, the boundaries between my mental and physical training began to collapse. I became more concerned with my state of mind than with external results. I practiced what I'd learned from *The Inner Game of Tennis*—non-judgmental awareness through concentration, and simply paying attention to my body on the court.

Non-judgmental awareness can be confused with detachment, or not really caring what happens. But Gallwey makes a necessary distinction: "By ending judgment, you do not avoid seeing what is. Ending judgment means you neither add nor subtract from the facts before your eyes. Things appear as they are—undistorted. In this way, the mind becomes more calm."

As I went through my shooting workouts, or when I played in open gyms, I still paid attention to the results of my shot, but my attitude toward the results changed. When I missed, instead of letting myself get frustrated, I simply noted in my mind "missed short," or "missed long," or "missed flat."

When I made a shot, instead of swelling with pride, I made a note of "back rim make," or "perfect swish." Then I tried to turn my attention to the next play. I wasn't always successful, because my emotional state had been deeply conditioned to react strongly to unfolding results, but with time I noticed my ego mind (Self 1) quieting, and the part of me that knew how to knock down shots (Self 2) starting to take over.

9

During a layover in the Seattle airport I thought I recognized a woman sitting a few seats away from me. We made eye contact and waved, and then I went over to sit next to her. It was Libby Edson, who lives in my hometown. She's the founder of YoMind, an excellent organization that now brings Yoga and mindfulness education and training to kids and young adults across America.

Libby knew me from high school, and she asked how my college career was going. When I told her that it hadn't been going very well, but that I'd begun meditating, she invited me to practice yoga and mindfulness with her over the summer. So I practiced yoga with her at least twice per week, and she helped me develop my mindfulness practice in conjunction with the yoga. Her patience and wisdom were invaluable. I stayed in touch with her throughout my senior season, and we've become good friends.

My mental struggles on the court in college were due in part to my false perceptions regarding both activities and people. I waited for things to "matter" before I bothered trying to do my best. When there were people around that I wanted to impress, like my coach, or the upperclassmen on the team, or a pretty girl at a party, I felt intense pressure to perform—pressure that produced anxiety and self-doubt. Alone in my room with nobody watching, I often let myself slide into the modern mental fog of mindlessly scrolling my phone for hours. I thought that if nobody saw me, it didn't matter what I did.

One of the most important concepts that Libby emphasizes is this mantra: "How you do anything is how you do everything." She encouraged me not to wait until I was on the court or the yoga mat or the meditation chair to cultivate mindful attention. She argued that it's a mistake to discriminate between activities, and to try to turn our mindfulness practice on and off. Whether it's a hike in nature, a trip to the DMV, or a playoff game, we should do our best to cultivate mindful attention.

When I understood that I couldn't simply turn on a healthy attitude in big moments, I began practicing healthy mental states for their own sake instead of as a means to attain external success and status. It became clear that how I behaved eating lunch in the cafeteria actually related to my mental state in the final minutes of a close game.

10

A few weeks before heading back to Regis I'd enjoyed a meal with my grandparents. After dinner, Opa handed me a small hardcover book, tan with red trim. I opened it up to find the title: *Meditations by Marcus Aurelius.* Accustomed to flashy books with clickbait titles and subtitles, I found the simplicity of this book appealing. It looked and felt like something important.

I soon learned that Marcus Aurelius was a Roman Emperor in the second century who practiced Stoic philosophy. *Meditations* (not to be confused with "meditation" as I've described it) is a collection of entries from his private journal—brief bits of advice to himself influenced by his Stoicism.

As I read, I was surprised by the similarities between Aurelius's Stoicism and what I'd been practicing since my diagnosis as a sophomore. He focused on his own attitude: "Seek what is in harmony with your own nature and strive towards this, even if it brings no reputation; for every man is allowed to seek his own good."

He focuses on reducing self-serving desires, and facing the uncertainty of the future with bravery: "No longer be pulled by the strings like a puppet by self seeking impulse, no longer be either dissatisfied with your present lot, or shrink from the future."

He warns against worrying about the behaviors and opinions of others. Instead, we should focus on our own actions and character. "How much trouble he avoids who does not look to see what his neighbor says or does or thinks, but only to what he does himself, that it may be just and pure; or as Agathon says, look not round at the depraved morals of others, but run straight along the line without deviating from it."

He constantly reminds himself of his own mortality, that his time is limited. Athletes can benefit from his message by reminding themselves that their playing career is brief, and that the end of a career is a kind of death. "Do not act as if you would live ten thousand years. Death hangs over you. While you live, while it is in your power, be good."

He believes that character is measured by where people place their attention. "Your duty in the midst of such things is to show good humor and not a proud air; and to understand that a man is worth just as much as the things about which he busies himself."

Reading Marcus Aurelius, I understood that useful advice for athletes—for anybody—can come from long ago with origins in distant places. His guidance offered both psychological relief and an updated mental framework that helped me understand my final season.

In the previous three summers, my return to Denver had always produced anxiety. Leaving the freedom and peace of my hometown for the pressure and stress of college basketball threw my mind out of balance. Before my senior year I did my best to absorb what I was reading from Aurelius and what I was practicing on the meditation chair. I concentrated on my own attitudes and actions without shrinking from the uncertainty of the future.

I boarded my flight to Denver with newly acquired peace and resolve. Throughout my senior year I read a page or two of *Meditations* every night before bed, or whenever I felt I needed a mental course correction. Reading this passage before practices and games always helped point my mind in the right direction:

"Every moment think steadily as a Roman and as a man to do what you have in hand with perfect and simple dignity, and kindliness, and freedom, and justice; and to give yourself relief from all other thoughts. And you will give yourself relief, if you do every act of your life as if it were the last, renouncing all carelessness and passionate resistance to the commands of reason, and all hypocrisy, and self-love, and discontent with the portion which has been given to you. You see how few the things are which a man needs to lay hold of in order to live a life which flows in quiet, and is like the life of the gods; for the gods on their part will require nothing more from him who observes these things."

CHAPTER 14

NEW CULTURE

1

When I returned to campus I discovered a brand new team culture: a new coaching staff paired with many new players, and a system radically different than the one I was used to. Our preseason workouts and practices were intense, demanding, and well structured. Each drill and workout was set up as a competition, and each player's winning percentage, tracked as we competed in drills and scrimmages, was kept and posted in the locker room. Going through the motions and waiting for practice to end wasn't a viable option.

Beyond the increased workload in basketball, I took three upper division math classes in the first semester. My days were busy and productive, with little time for self pity. I bounced from one activity to the next, and I had to bring energy and attention to whatever I was doing to avoid falling behind.

I wasn't confident about competing successfully with teammates for spots in the playing rotation, but I worked hard in the drills and in the weight workouts, and immediately felt appreciated for my efforts by the new staff. They valued toughness and consistency, things I knew I could control and bring every day.

2

A shot tracking chart with each team member's name hung in the locker room. We were given the goal of making 3,000 shots per month outside of practice, about 100 makes per day. Assistant coaches were available at almost any time to rebound for us if we came in to shoot alone. One afternoon I went to the gym to get some shots up. When I walked into the coaches' office to ask an assistant to rebound, I found Coach Brady there alone. I was still hesitant around him, afraid of saying or doing the wrong thing.

"What's up, Billy?" he said, without looking up from the notepad on his desk.

"Oh, hey, Coach, I was going to shoot and I'll just go do it on my own."

He dropped his pencil, sprung up from his desk and said, "I've got a few minutes."

My heart began to race. If I'd known the head coach would be my rebounder I'd never have come to the gym. This felt like a final exam instead of a low-key workout before weight training. But before my anxiety could take over I placed my attention on my feet on the floor, and on the physical sensations in my chest, and then told myself to face this challenge with courage.

Coach Brady is a short, slender and fit man with a chiseled and intense face. He speaks and walks with authority and has an infectious energy that demands respect. I started nervously, shooting a few mid-range jumpers before moving out to the three-point line. Then Brady took over, leading me from spot to spot. He hurried after rebounds and snapped chest passes until he was sweating, talking to me and pushing me to be focused and to work toward improved consistency, making every rep count. Soon I was immersed in the drill, and was snapping the net from all over the court. I was happy and excited showing him what I could do.

After swishing my final shot from my final spot Coach came over and gave me a fist bump. He began talking to me about things I should work on to get myself ready for games. I was surprised that a head coach would do this for a player who likely wouldn't contribute much during the season. Maybe I really did have a chance to play.

3

It felt strange for a college basketball team to be practicing the same skills I'd worked on in 5th grade—how to pass, catch, and pivot. The new coaching staff seemed obsessed with fundamental skills, and we performed countless repetitions of the basics, and were expected to incorporate them into our competitive drills. If a player didn't pivot with his inside foot and create space, the entire offensive team was punished by losing possession of the ball. This exposed something important about my game. My old habit was to catch a pass and immediately raise the ball over my head, allowing the defender to climb into my space and force me to play backward. Every time I did it Coach blew the whistle and gave the ball to the other team.

Embarrassed and frustrated, I had to make a change. I started catching the ball and ripping forward hard, creating space on the court. This put me in a much better position to make a pass, and I felt generally better on the court. In my previous three seasons I'd been psychologically tor-mented by defenders, because whenever I caught the ball I was forced back on my heels and had to make a quick, safe pass so as not to turn the ball over.

When I watch old high school videos I get uncom-fortable seeing myself tossing weak passes with too much arc. I usually got away with it against the soft defenses I faced, but in college my weak passes were often deflected or stolen. The result was that I usually resorted to a safe pass directed away from the basket.

My new coaches made me learn how to use my lower body, to zip the ball low and hard across the court to the outside hand of the recipient. When I did this I felt confident and present on the court. I felt like I belonged. Lacking fundamental skills was at the root of my anxiety issues in college basketball.

4

In high school I was something of a star, hitting three-point-ers, driving to the basket, and coming off ball screens and making plays for others. The idea in my head was that I had to keep doing all of that at the college level. For most of my first three years I tried to improve in all areas of guard play, and I underperformed at most of them.

In an early preseason scrimmage as a senior, I drove to the basket multiple times. On one occasion I floated a layup over a post player and scored, but my other attempts failed. I got my shot swatted out of bounds more than once and then heard the standard "Get that shit out!" from the shot-blocker. I also pump-faked and took a dribble into the paint and missed a push shot. I finished the scrimmage convinced I wouldn't earn playing time.

After the scrimmage Coach Brady told me to stop driving to the basket against big, athletic defenders. He didn't want me shooting pull-up mid-range jumpers either. This came as an uncomfortable surprise. I'd spent a lot of time working on my dribble-drive moves and my mid-range game, and now I wasn't supposed to use them. But before long I understood that simplifying my role allowed me to succeed. Coach stopped having any ball screens set for me, and told me that when I caught a pass I should shoot, shot-fake, or pass, to keep the offense moving. In my individual workouts I stopped practicing ball screen reads, floaters, and intricate finishes over defenders, and instead worked on movement without the ball, shooting from deep, and shot-fakes with side-dribble three-pointers. I'd become a specialist.

My simplified, well-defined role gave me a sense of purpose every day at practice and in games. Instead of just trying to "play well," or "play better," which had been my goals for years, I knew exactly how to contribute value to my tribe: bring a sense of toughness and leadership to the court, space the offense, and knock down open threes. I had a useful and satisfying role.

5

"You can be as quiet off the court as you like, but when you step on the court quietness isn't allowed." When Coach Brady said this at our first workout with him, I felt both resistance and nervousness. Throughout my career I'd kept quiet on the court. The most I'd ever done was call out ball screens, and clap for teammates from the bench after good plays.

Forcing myself to yell out commands had always felt awkward. When Coach told us that we weren't allowed to be quiet, I dreaded the idea of faking enthusiasm, and yelling useless clichés to teammates after their good plays. Even in Little League I'd hated organized cheers and chants, because they felt forced and artificial.

But I soon learned that Coach Brady's mandatory communication was different, and I learned to appreciate it. Coach encouraged us to communicate constantly, with loud and demonstrative voices. During dead balls we all came together at the free throw line to make sure that everybody was on the same page about what we were running. This commitment to communication was a major factor in our improvement as a team.

In my junior season I became dedicated to my meditation practice, and while it helped me a lot, I made a mistake in the way I tried to bring it with me to the court. My confusion was thinking that in order to be mindful on the court I had to be quiet and calm. Ironically, trying to be mindful sometimes took me away from the flow state athletes know and love. Instead of becoming immersed in the game, I was consciously trying to be mindful, which turned me into an actor playing the part of a calm, composed athlete.

When I was forced out of my shell, I experienced an important shift in how I felt on the court. Communicating while I played took me out of my head and let me sink into the present moment. I soon embraced my new persona, and ended up communicating constantly.

Aside from loud communication, I continued to find more of a presence on the court and in the locker room. Sometimes I got into yelling matches with my teammates in intense drills and scrimmages. In previous years I would have tried to make peace as quickly as possible, but I no longer backed down from challenges.

My mindfulness practice helped me to keep the anger I experienced under control, and I could usually remain calm and focused in the midst of conflict and shit-talking. It was through this experience that I realized that meditation wasn't making me a harmless pushover, but was allowing me to be true to myself. I could become mindful of my discomfort with conflict, and instead of reacting to it, I could refocus my attention on the game without backing down. My teammates still liked me, and I felt a new level of respect in the locker room.

Being loud and demonstrative, embracing challenges and conflict, and focusing on the current play immersed me in the game and left no room for thoughts about me or how I was doing.

Golden State's surly Draymond Green is the perfect villain for me as a sports fan, and I enjoy cheering against him, but I can't help but be impressed when I watch him compete. He constantly barks out commands and relevant advice to his teammates. And while sometimes his emotions get the best of him, it's clear that he's fully into the competition, with no concerns other than getting the best of his opponent on the current play.

CHAPTER 15

LOVE AND LUCK

1

I saw beautiful women on campus every week, women I hardly ever saw at house parties and bars. On Tuesdays and Thursdays after lunch I often saw Rebecca sitting on a bench outside the cafeteria with some friends. Her beauty was intimidating. She's a first-generation Ethiopian American, with long legs and perfectly lovely dark skin. She had her own unique style in fashion, and always looked just right. It took a while, but I finally worked up enough nerve to approach her.

As I headed out of the cafeteria I told myself I'd talk to her if she was sitting outside on a bench. When I pushed the doors open, there she was, with four other women. Pressure rose in my chest, my heart rate doubled, and I tried to invent a reason for not going through with it. But my body was moving in her direction, and then we made eye contact. If I veered away I'd never generate the nerve I needed.

Walking towards the group, I did my best to look self-assured, confident. Should I address all five women, or just Rebecca? I said hi to everyone before I spoke directly to her. When we exchanged some pleasantries about how our summers had gone I told her about my time in Peru. Then I suggested that we hang out sometime and "catch up," which felt stupid as soon as I said it. We weren't old friends and had no need to catch up on anything. I'd set myself up to be publicly rejected. But she agreed. I handed her my phone so she could type in her number, said good-bye to the group, and walked away in a daze.

I'd been admiring Rebecca from a distance for nearly four years, secretly wanting to ask her for a date, and I found myself relating that fact to what had happened to me in basketball. Sometimes we have to risk failure to succeed.

On our first date I took Rebecca to the book bar near campus. She looked stunning, and I was nervous, but thankfully the skills I'd learned for dealing with unease on the basketball court seemed to work here too. My anxiety subsided as we fell into conversation. We talked for three hours without interruption. She was smart, funny, gentle, and impressively self-assured. On our drive back to her apartment I asked her to plug in her phone and play some music, and the first song she picked was "Average Joe" by Kendrick Lamar—a niche rap song that I loved, and that only rap music fans with good taste cared about. Next came a blues-rock song by The White Stripes that I'd never heard but liked immediately.

After dropping Rebecca off I felt intensely happy, something far beyond ego or validation. I was grateful for time spent with her, and the concept of falling in love made perfect sense—it really did feel like I was falling, whether I wanted to or not.

2

"The ability to be friends with a woman, particularly the woman you love, is to me the greatest achievement. In all my life I have only known a few couples that were friends as well as lovers."

– Henry Miller, *On Turning Eighty*

Friday and Saturday nights of too much beer and loud noise were replaced by peaceful nights with a girlfriend who wasn't into partying much either. We went to concerts, out to dinner, watched *Curb Your Enthusiasm*, and always enjoyed our time together. Through long days on the court and in the library I found myself looking forward to spending time with Rebecca.

For years I'd been influenced by beliefs held by many members of my generation—that monogamy was unnatural, marriage was a trap, having kids was unethical, and more. Some of my male friends ridiculed traditional relationships, and some female friends claimed they never wanted a family. I listened to self-help gurus on YouTube pointing out everything that's supposedly wrong with a committed relationship and claiming that sexual variety is the number one goal of romantic life. This produced fantasies of being rich and single, traveling the world, and meeting beautiful women everywhere.

I don't think being in a long-term relationship is always better than being single. There's an over-supply of bad relationships, maybe especially in high schools and colleges. Some of my teammates were in destructive relationships and seemed tortured by them, and their college experiences and basketball careers suffered as a result.

But I'd been blind to how a relationship that worked could improve my life. Rebecca's energy was refreshing. She's a genuinely happy and decent person whose positive qualities seem to rub off on people she's with. She has no interest at all in sports, and it was nice being with someone who liked me for reasons that had nothing to do with basketball. Her apartment was clean and well decorated, and she took the time to water plants and light candles in the evenings—an oasis from my messy apartment and the stuffy gyms and locker rooms I spent so much of my time in. When I was there I forgot all about my shooting percentages and my upcoming math tests.

After spending time with her I felt energized about basketball and my classes, and life in general, and I liked who I became when I was with her, with no feeling that I needed to change anything. I could just be me.

I found myself in a happy relationship as soon as I became happy myself. And I knew how lucky I was.

CHAPTER 16

BETTER HABITS

1

So each day I made sure to practice my meditation for at least 20 minutes. Some days I found time to sit twice. Before practices and math tests I breathed deep, centering belly breaths, which calmed my nervous system. When I lay down at night to fall asleep I gently scanned my body before following my breaths until I dozed off.

Along with increased confidence and joy on the court, I was surprised to notice another consequential benefit— my priorities began changing. For the first time in my life I became drawn to simplicity. Instead of wanting to be stimulated, excited, distracted, and entertained, I wanted peace, calm, and a clear mind. Walking across campus from one class to another, I found myself organically noticing the beauty of the trees and the clouds, and feeling satisfied with life for no particular reason.

"FOMO"—the fear of missing out—is a widespread phenomenon in our 21st century culture, and it's all too common on college campuses. I felt it on many nights when I went to bed early and sober before a practice or game, knowing parties were happening. Missing out on something that my classmates were enjoying made me jealous. Then, as a senior, the experience turned itself around. I was satisfied and in fact felt relieved to be spending a quiet night with my friend and roommate.

Many of my former desires and impulses had been harmful, leading to temporary jolts of pleasure, distraction, and entertainment, but ultimately to suffering. I sought highs that came with subsequent lows. Joseph Goldstein writes this in *Mindfulness - A Practical Guide to Awakening*:

> "...our aim shouldn't be to follow the heart, but to train the heart. All of us have a mix of motivations; not everything in our hearts is wise or wholesome. The great power of mindful discernment allows us to abandon what is unwholesome and cultivate the good. This discernment is of inestimable value for our happiness and wellbeing."

2

Since high school I'd known that to feel and perform my best, sleep, nutrition, and hydration were important. But it wasn't until I developed a mindfulness meditation practice that I was able to truly commit to these things. I became mindful of my experience day to day, and I noticed what habits and behaviors were improving my life, and those that were diminishing it.

I realized that grabbing a few slices of pizza in the cafeteria wouldn't be worth the brain fog and lethargy I'd feel during the difficult workout I had coming in the afternoon. Choosing grilled chicken, salad and sweet potato for lunch required less willpower as a senior, because I appreciated mental clarity more than jolts of temporary pleasure.

I became acutely aware of how sleep affected my mood, my cognitive abilities, and my strength and endurance. In years prior, feeling tired, stressed, and lazy led me to want a release through alcohol or junk food. As a senior, all I needed was a good night of sober sleep.

I no longer allowed myself to study late into the night, and this forced me to spend my time more productively throughout the day. Knowing that I couldn't study until 1 a.m. meant that I had to put my phone away and work without distraction. Five hours of studying mixed with Youtube and Snapchat became two hours of focused work.

On my best nights, I put my phone away an hour before bed, and rather than looking at a screen I did some reading before I went to sleep. This routine helped produce deep, restful sleep. Sleep expert Mathew Walker claims that "Sleep is the greatest legal performance enhancing drug that most people are probably neglecting in sport." In his book *Why We Sleep,* Walker cites evidence that adequate sleep (8-10 hours of restful sleep) is crucial for skill development, endurance, strength, durability, testosterone levels, mood, and emotional regulation.

Many in athletic culture think that sleeping less demonstrates strength and toughness, presumably creating more time for useful productivity. I've heard athletes, coaches, motivational speakers and tech folks brag about how they get by with four or five hours of sleep per night. Apparently they regard sleep as an opportunity cost, and the logic appears to make sense—while everyone else sleeps comfortably for eight hours, I'll rip myself out of bed after five hours and have three extra hours of productivity. This is supposed to be seen as a sacrifice leading toward success, something like grabbing a kale salad instead of a cheeseburger.

But this is misguided and dangerous behavior. I think writer Maria Popova gives the perfect advice: "Be as religious and disciplined about your sleep as you are about your work. We tend to wear our ability to get by on little sleep as some sort of badge of honor that validates our work ethic. But what it really is is a profound failure of self-respect and of priorities. What could possibly be more important than your health and your sanity, from which all else springs?"

Of all the changes I made as a senior, my commitment to restful sleep was the most impactful. Creating firm boundaries to protect my sleep turned me into an entirely different player and person.

3

**"The modern struggle is fighting
weaponized addiction."**

- Naval Ravikant

My therapist told me that spending time away from my phone would likely help me resolve my issues with anxiety and depression. Along with fragmenting my attention, she pointed out that virtually everyone out there is broadcasting a happy, successful life on the internet, and that I might be contributing to my own gloom by scrolling Instagram and constantly seeing people who look happier than I am. Even though I understood her advice, I was too addicted to take it.

My mental training helped with this too, as I paid attention to my impulses to distract myself with a phone.

When stuck on a math problem, I reflexively picked up my phone for a quick hit of entertainment, and sometimes fell into a zombie-like trance. After a Youtube video of Damian Lillard highlights, another video that seemed irresistible was offered, and then another, and another, endlessly. Sometimes half an hour went by before I got back to the math problem.

We tend to think that platforms like Facebook, Instagram, and Twitter are free, and that we're the lucky customers who get to use them. The truth is that advertisers are the customers of Facebook, Instagram, Twitter, and Youtube, and we're the product. Our habits and behavior are collected and sold, and hugely profitable companies thrive because of the amount of time we spend on their carefully manipulated platforms. The more we scroll and click, and the more ads we see, the more money they make, enabling them to keep making matters worse.

We have what design ethicist Tristan Harris calls "the attention economy," where companies like Facebook, Instagram (owned by Facebook), Twitter, and Snapchat compete to grab and keep user attention. Teams of software engineers work tirelessly to make their products as addictive as possible. An athlete who wants to balance training, homework, physical therapy, extra practice and a social life needs to be able to study and train without distractions, but carrying around a literal distraction machine makes this nearly impossible.

As a senior, I drastically reduced the time I spent on social media and my smartphone. When I did homework I turned the phone off and put it in my bag, out of sight. Before bed I turned it to Do Not Disturb and put it far away from me so that it wouldn't wake me at night, and so I wasn't tempted to begin my morning by scrolling.

4

My only previous attempts to quit drinking heavily had been desperate efforts to gain an advantage over my teammates, and to feel superior to my friends. But when I didn't feel any less anxious and unhappy, I soon found myself tipping back a cheap bottle of vodka. When I stopped drinking too much for the sake of mental clarity, it worked. I still went to occasional parties, and enjoyed myself.

Heavy drinkers often try to talk non-drinkers into joining their club. Dionte, a senior when I was a freshman, was an interesting example. Every Saturday after our last practice of the week we'd badger him in the locker room about not drinking with us. He was a great player and loved the sport, and was also passionate about music and making beats. Many of the "pre-games" were held at his house, so while we drank we'd hear the ceaseless thumping of his beats coming from his room for hours on end. He'd come out once in a while to check in, and never seemed to cast judgment. He'd simply say hi, then return to his room and continue making beats.

While I joined my teammates in giving him grief for not wanting to drink and party, and in pretending our behavior was the only way to go, I was in fact impressed with Dionte's self assurance. It's no surprise to me that he now has a fine job in L. A. with Apple Music, is still in great physical shape, and writes poetry as a serious hobby. Now I see him as an example of someone smart enough and strong enough to think for himself.

Another important finding from Mathew Walker's book is how detrimental alcohol is for adequate sleep and recovery. When we go to bed drunk, we generally fall asleep quickly, and we're in a senseless state that gives the illusion of sound sleep, when it's actually sedation. Alcohol blocks the brain from the deep stages of sleep essential for recovery and health, and habitual drinking makes adequate sleep impossible. Alcohol before bed might help one fall asleep faster, but it blocks the brain from the deep sleep athletes need for recovery and skill development.

Too much alcohol has detrimental effects on muscle recovery. Muscles don't grow during workouts in the weight room, they're broken down, and recover and grow later during periods of rest. If an athlete's only day of rest is spent recovering from last night's alcohol, muscles don't properly recover. Without getting drunk every weekend, my progress in the gym and in the weight room went better than ever before.

5

People from cultures around the world have used alcohol as a bonding agent for thousands of years, and, today, going out to bars and parties can be an enjoyable and beneficial activity for young people—an opportunity to develop social skills, and to create lasting bonds with close friends. When a sports team parties together it can reduce inhibitions and build comradery, chemistry, and trust.

Some parents and coaches try to convince athletes that they should avoid partying, drugs, and alcohol in high school and college. This is well-intentioned theoretical advice, but it's about as helpful as promoting sexual abstinence until marriage. Drugs and alcohol are readily available in nearly all high schools and colleges, and most students, athletes among them, experiment with various substances.

I don't think trying to abstain altogether from drugs and partying is necessary or wise. Some of my favorite college memories were from wild nights out with my friends. Early in the Regis school year the process of teammates bonding while drinking together was beneficial, up to a point. The law of diminishing returns set in when the ritual continued weekend after weekend. The development of chemistry stalled, and hangovers and lack of sleep compounded.

I remember stumbling through too many cold winter nights with my other drinking teammates, hunting for the most enjoyable party with the prettiest girls. Seeing myself in the mirror of a restroom often cut through the drunken fog and produced an unpleasant clarity. The glossed over eyes and bright red cheeks I saw weren't really me. I knew I was doing this to myself, weekend after weekend, as a way to run from my own unhappiness. I suspected that some of my friends felt the same way, and I was surprised that Tolstoy's description of a college party from his 1856 novel *Childhood, Boyhood, and Youth* related directly to my experience:

"But above all I remember that throughout the whole evening I constantly felt that I was acting very stupidly, pretending to be having a very good time, pretending to be very keen on drinking and acting as though it never even occurred to me that I was drunk; and I felt all the time that others, pretending just the same, were also acting very stupidly. It seemed to me that each one individually found it as unpleasant as I did, but in the belief that he was the only one who had this feeling of unpleasantness, considered himself bound to pretend he was having a good time so as not to spoil the general merriment."

The same basic principle applies to marijuana, which is in fact relatively harmless in moderation, but, as with alcohol, is often abused. It's typical for a young athlete who enjoys smoking pot to want to smoke whenever possible—before eating, before training, before class, before bed—which is clearly not a healthful way to live.

Pot is often used as a way to wind down at the end of the day, calm anxiety, and help the user fall asleep. Matthew Walker concludes that getting high before bed blocks the critical deep sleep vital for emotional regulation, leaving users anxious and depressed the following day, and therefore tempted to self-medicate again with cannabis. This becomes a cycle in which the perceived remedy actually causes the problem it's meant to solve. So while a habit of smoking pot is undoubtedly less physically destructive than a habit of drinking too much alcohol, athletes who go to bed high night after night deprive themselves of the principal benefits of deep sleep: enhanced skill development and increased endurance.

6

I'm not recommending that young athletes become obsessively disciplined regarding drugs and partying. An inevitable part of growing up is the freedom to explore, and sometimes make mistakes. Those who never allow themselves to make a mistake or an unfortunate decision are missing out on something necessary. As Nassim Taleb put it in *The Bed of Procrustes*, "Wisdom in the young is as unattractive as frivolity in the elderly."

But too many young athletes derail their careers when they take it too far, either by making one huge, life altering mistake, or by slowly sabotaging their careers over time. Even in the midst of wild, rebellious behavior, there have to be boundaries set that are never to be crossed: Driving drunk, unprotected sex with a new partner, sex without clear consent, taking drugs that haven't been tested for purity, etc. It's important to remember that a small risk, when taken repeatedly, becomes a huge risk (a 5% risk repeated 20 times becomes a 64% risk). You surely don't have to risk your entire career, or your future, or the health and safety of others, in order to have fun.

Young people trying to justify questionable behavior tend to tell themselves comforting lies. I've often heard and sometimes used these rationalizations myself:

"I'll stop smoking pot every day when school starts again."

"I'll stop drinking every weekend when games start."

"I'll wear a condom next time."

"I'll stop taking unprescribed Adderall next semester."

These promises aren't always kept. Abstinence from partying and impulsive behavior isn't necessary for a young athlete, but no relationship with drugs, alcohol, and partying should interfere with a healthy, sustainable lifestyle.

CHAPTER 17

MENTAL BALANCE

1

**"I am here today to cross the swamp,
not to fight all the alligators."**

—Rosamund Stone Zander in *The Art of Possibility*

A successful student athlete's career includes making small, correct decisions over and over again: getting to bed sober and on time, paying attention in classes, sitting down to meditate instead of scrolling Instagram, etc. These efforts won't earn praise or immediate reward, but the right decisions build momentum resulting in necessary improvements.

With an improved sleep routine, diet, and relationship with alcohol and my phone, I became a new person as a senior. I faced problems but was less threatened by them and enjoyed a sense of mental stability. For the first time in my career I didn't dread hearing the alarm go off. I had a disciplined routine and lived with a pervasive sense of satisfaction.

And I also enjoyed myself, which was important. Unlike previous years, my routine was pleasant and sustainable. Yes, sometimes I had to summon some willpower to make a skillful choice, but I wasn't my own slave, forcing myself to do things all day long, and I tried not to criticize myself when I didn't follow my routine perfectly—I just got back on track, again and again.

The unfortunate mindset I recognized in myself early on was that of a suffering athlete trying to deal with failure by sacrificing virtually everything else in life as a means toward improvement—a rigid discipline that becomes an identity.

Some of the desperate plans I made as a sophomore were absurd. I thought that abstinence from what I enjoyed would make me "deserve" to play well and earn the respect of the coaching staff. If I made enough sacrifices, the universe would have to reward me. My behavior was self-flagellation, the religious ritual of whipping oneself to please God in the hopes of earning a better life.

Trying to religiously commit to a rigid set of rules and principles as a way to find security and relief is a common tendency. In *Childhood, Boyhood, and Youth*, Nikolenka tries to solve his own adolescent problems by "...writing down a list of my daily tasks and duties which should last me all my life, together with a statement of my life's aim, and the rules by which I meant unswervingly to be guided." I laughed as I read this, remembering how many times I'd made, and broken, the same commitment.

Applying extreme remedies is always tough, so difficult that most of us eventually give up until another idea, another wave of inspiration washes over us. What's ironic about this process is that renouncing temporary pleasures is a temporary pleasure in itself. When we make promises to ourselves and enjoy anticipating how much better the future will be, we ignore how difficult the promises can be to keep. A failure to live up to our impossibly high standards then results in more pain and disappointment. Nikolenka's commitment to his new, rigid life lasted only until a line he drew on the paper to organize the various sections came out crooked. He debated starting over, and then was called downstairs by his father, and never looked at the list again.

Yes, coaches appreciate players who make personal sacrifices for the sake of improvement, and they appreciate players who show up on time every day and bring consistent effort and energy. What they appreciate most, barring any truly awful behavior, are the players who give the team the best chance to win.

Nervous, over-thinking athletes want to believe that the more they suffer, the more likely they are to play well. But usually they suffer for the sake of suffering. Allen Iverson was notorious for blowing off practice, and staying at the clubs late into the nights before games. Undoubtedly most if not all of his teammates showed up every day ready to practice hard and compete, and were well rested before games. Yet, year after year, Iverson was among the league leaders in minutes played. Dennis Rodman, the Hall of Fame power forward who won five championships with the Pistons and the Bulls, lived a wild life off the court. He once missed a practice during the NBA Finals because he flew across the country to party and participate in a pro wrestling event. These wild lifestyles aren't what we should emulate, but they serve as reminders that, in the end, the best players play.

Occasionally the free and relaxed spirit of an athlete who isn't doing "everything right" can correlate with superior attitude and confidence on the court or the field.

An athlete's behavior should be whatever maximizes the chance of playing well and enjoying it. Sometimes that can mean sleeping in an extra hour, or spending a relaxed evening with friends, or going out on Saturday night for a break in the routine.

2

"Neither in your actions be sluggish nor in your conversation without method, nor wandering in thought, nor let there be in your soul either inward contention or external effusion; nor in life be so busy as to have no leisure."

- Marcus Aurelius

When I'm thinking rationally I understand that gradual progress over a long period of time leads to better results than short, anxiety-fueled attempts at improvement. This isn't a recommendation for laziness, or for giving less than full effort. It's an acknowledgment that gradual and achievable improvements are enjoyable and yield results superior to the frantic work ethic that self-help gurus and coaches sometimes recommend.

Early on in my college career, my tendency was to try to add things to my already busy schedule, as a way to be more productive, often sacrificing sleep and necessary rest as a result. As a senior, instead of adding more activities to a busy schedule, I cultivated intensity and awareness in shorter, more productive periods. I realized that shooting for 30 minutes mindfully and without distraction does more good than shooting for two hours with 60% focus and energy. Studying hard for ninety minutes with unbroken attention before enjoying a meal with friends does more good than a four hour mix of Instagram, studying, and texting friends.

3

"There is no more miserable human being than one in whom nothing is habitual but indecision."

- William James, The Principles of Psychology

Instead of struggling with ourselves everyday, and relying on constant willpower to make intelligent decisions, we should establish positive habits and routines that make good decisions easy. For instance, the habit of keeping your phone away from your bed and not checking it until you've completed a morning routine will set you up for better days, and therefore a better career. Whatever it is you want to do (get extra work in, go to physical therapy, study without distraction, etc) it's much easier and more pleasant to establish a habit than to rely on your own will power to make new, good decisions day after day.

Most athletes have goals, like making the starting line up, earning a scholarship, making all-conference, going pro overseas, or getting into an elite graduate school. Goals can be helpful motivators, but it's your daily habits that most often determine where you end up. Your actions in the present moment sow the seeds of your future. And it's important that your habits and routines leave time for leisure and spontaneity.

It was my experience that a meditation practice helped me resonate with healthier habits and behaviors, and allowed me to establish a happier, more productive life.

CHAPTER 18

THE BLUE TEAM

1

"'It's only a game' is a saying we can apply once the event is over, but not before."

- Hans Ulrich Gumbrecht, *In Praise of Athletic Beauty*

As the season approached Coach split the team into the Whites and Blues. The Blue team was rated by the coaches as the best seven players at the time. The division was meant to foster competition, with no spot guaranteed to last. Coach called off the names, and to my great surprise "Hansen" was the final name he called on the Blue team. I'd be in the playing rotation for our first game. I was excited, and at the same time worried about squandering my opportunity.

David Whyte's poem "The Bell and the Blackbird" describes an Irish monk standing near his monastery and hearing two beautiful sounds at the same time: a reverberating bell in the church, and a blackbird out in the forest. The sound of the bell is calling the monk to prayer—to more depth and preparation for the world. The call of the blackbird is inviting the monk to go out into the world just as he finds it, and it finds him. I think his poem relates to training and performing in sports.

Before our first game I felt nervous about the call to perform. I knew that I had much more progress to make with my mental and physical training, but I also knew it was time to show up and use all the mental and physical skills I had at hand. When you compete in a game, you do it regardless of any physical or mental limitations or liabilities. As the competition finds you, you play as well as you can, understanding that your game, and your mind, will never be perfect.

We played a non-conference match-up against Lubbock Christian. Sitting in the locker room before tipoff I was nervous to the point of near nausea, but it wasn't anywhere near as debilitating as the nervousness of years past, when I didn't want to set foot on the court. After my pregame meditation, visualization, and the breathing exercises Libby had taught me, I felt centered despite the anxiety.

Coach called my name six minutes into the first half, and as I ran to the scorer's table the anxiety returned. Out on the court I could move my hands and breathe freely, but I started off tentatively, afraid of making mistakes or missing shots. I ended up playing 17 minutes, taking two tentative shots and missing both. I thought I'd squandered my chance, but in our second game I was still in the rotation and knocked down some shots. Scoring meaningful points in meaningful minutes was rewarding.

2

After Sunday off we returned to practice on Monday, and everyone involved shared a sense of urgency and obvious frustration after two losses. When Coach split up the teams I was in the top five, so I'd soon make the first start of my college career. The starting guards hadn't played well in our losses, so, given my habitual negative state of mind and the lingering imposter syndrome, I wondered if starting me was meant to serve as a tool to motivate them. The last three years had conditioned me to expect failure. I wasn't convinced that Coach might think I was his best option.

3

I made my first career start in our first win of the season, playing a solid 26 minutes. We won again in our fourth game, and I played decently, knocking down a few more threes. I was elated to have contributed to two preseason wins as a starter.

But during the next two games I played timidly, taking only seven shots and scoring only seven points. After another tentative performance in our conference opener I fell out of the starting lineup. But I bounced back with a good game off the bench in our first conference victory, and was back in the top five. Then, in the final three games before Christmas break, I scored a total of three points and took only five shots. I was still afraid of making mistakes. Scoring was how I could help the team, and in games when I didn't score I was benched in the second half because there were better options than me on defense. We left for Christmas break disappointed as a group after starting conference play with one win and four losses.

4

I was only mildly satisfied with my first semester. I'd made the starting lineup and contributed, and earned good grades again. I figured I might stay in the rotation through the season if I stayed tough and focused. There was a chance I'd be replaced in the starting lineup but, for the time being, I was playing. My anxiety was under control, and I was enjoying practices and games. My improved daily life led to greater physical energy and mental clarity.

Two nights before I flew back to Colorado, my Dad and I talked about the season. He told me he was thrilled to see me enjoying basketball. We talked about Regis' standing in the RMAC and our prospects of making the playoffs, and he questioned me about my coach and teammates. He'd recognized the flaw in my attitude on the court—my unwillingness to take risks, which led to my disappearing from the offense for extended periods. He understood that my fear of making mistakes was holding my game back, making me more likely to fail.

I resisted his analysis at first. I'd worked hard and made the starting lineup, and felt fairly comfortable with how the season was going. Then, when I returned to Colorado, I met with Coach Bergeson, who'd watched film of each player over the break. He echoed much of what my dad had said. He'd also noticed a subtle difference between how I shot the ball in drills as opposed to games. In drills, I shot "like I fucking meant it," raising up and snapping with confidence. In games I looked hesitant and afraid of getting my shot blocked. He said he'd rather have to tell me to stop taking bad shots than have to beg me to be aggressive.

Assistant coach Dan Snyder used something he knew would resonate with me—statistics. He pointed out that many shooters are too concerned about getting their shots blocked, leading to rushed, off-balance shots designed to get over defenders. He pointed out that if I stuck my nose into the shot, as if no one was closing out on me, I might get three or four shots blocked in the next 20 games, but I'd make many more shots as a result. If I didn't get any shots blocked, I wasn't shooting with conviction.

CHAPTER 19

LETTING IT FLY

1

Our first game after the break was an exhibition against Colorado State University. Exhibition games didn't count toward our record, and their stats didn't count toward our season totals. It was exciting to play against a Division 1 team in a large arena. I started, and, despite my commitment to be more aggressive, I began playing cautiously again.

A few minutes into the game a butt screen was called for our point guard, Noah, at the top of the key. It was my job to follow the screener, and then "fill" behind the screen, opposite the direction that Noah chose. When Noah broke to his right hand I sprinted the other way. My defender got caught by the roll man, Noah jump-stopped and delivered a chest pass to my shooting pocket. As I caught the ball my defender, a lanky Division 1 guard, was sprinting toward me. I started into my shot but I stopped it at the top, afraid my shot would be altered or blocked.

I swung the ball to the wing, who dumped the ball into the post. Our big guy was called for a travel as he started into his move. As I ran back down the court I heard "Bill!" coming from Noah. He waited until I met his eyes before he yelled: "Shoot the fucking ball!"

I finished my first stint on the court without taking a single shot. I didn't make any glaring errors, and didn't contribute much either, and came to the bench frustrated.

I checked back in determined to play aggressively, even if it meant making mistakes. After a long rebound I sprinted up the wing. Noah led me with a pass. I caught the ball and without hesitation rose up for three from beyond NBA range. It was a wild shot in transition that came up short. I ran back on defense, the game went on, and I wasn't benched.

A few possessions later Jarrett drove the baseline, and I filled the opposite baseline, giving him a safety valve as he ran into multiple defenders at the rim. As I caught his pass my feet were already moving towards the shot. I stuck my nose on the rim, released my follow through with conviction, and watched the ball snap through the net.

Then a crucial shift took place. For the first time in years, I felt a sense of confidence during a game, with no fear of making a mistake. I let myself play, feeling sure that if I had space I'd take shots and make them. It felt like I was playing outdoor pickup at laguna beach, only now I was in a D1 arena.

I checked out of the game with a few minutes remaining. We were down by 20 points and a win was beyond reach. As I walked off the court and sat down I realized that the usual undercurrent of self-evaluation and self-doubt had disappeared during the entire second half. I was sweating, tired and frustrated that we couldn't stop them on defense, but I was also satisfied. I had no idea how many shots I'd taken or how many points I'd scored. It had been the first genuine flow state I'd experienced during competition in years.

After the game I looked at the box score and saw that I'd finished with 9 points, 3-6 from the three point line. On the bus ride home my friend Dylan said playfully, "Young Hansen looked like he knew the stats didn't count tonight." He was referring to my unusually aggressive shot selection, and I laughed and answered sarcastically, but his comment revealed something important.

I'd kept close track of my shooting percentages up until that point in the season, and always had a running count of makes and misses during games. Knowing that stats didn't count in an exhibition game against a Division I school had apparently let me shoot as freely and aggressively as I did in pick-up games.

2

"The mass of men live lives of quiet desperation."

- Henry David Thoreau

Even though that had been my best game of the season, the bus ride home was painful. There was no hiding from it anymore. I'd been told by my Dad, my coaches, and my point guard, people I trusted and respected, to be more aggressive. I realized that until that game I'd spent much of my energy on the court trying to protect myself from failure. I was trying not to miss too many shots, guarding my precious statistics, trying not to disappoint my teammates. I wanted to control my experience on the court.

Did I really want to spend the final 20 games of my life avoiding mistakes, and trying to play just well enough to stay in the playing rotation? I realized that in order to make the most of my remaining games I'd need to push out of my comfort zone, and let myself become vulnerable to failure.

My Dad had posed the question over Christmas break—in the last 20 games of my life, would I rather err on the side of being too aggressive, or of trying to avoid mistakes? I finally knew the answer.

3

Our next game was a conference home game against Colorado State Pueblo. I showed up to the gym in the spirit of vulnerability and surrender. I decided that, just as I'd practiced on the meditation chair, I was going to let myself be vulnerable. Despite my nervousness I committed to taking risks, and to shoot whenever I had a legitimate opportunity. In our third possession down the court I caught a pass within the flow of the offense and, without much space away from my defender, went up aggressively and shot with conviction. I watched the ball float through the air and graze the back rim as it dropped through the net. I liked the feeling and wanted more.

A few possessions later we ran through our motion offense, with quick ball movement and hard cuts, but we didn't create an open shot. With 10 seconds left on the shot clock we called the same high butt screen pick-and-roll for Noah. He dribbled hard off the screen as our crowd counted down the seconds. When Noah hit a wall of defenders he flung the ball in my direction. I caught it well outside the three-point line with three seconds left on the clock, and heaved a shot from long range over the outstretched hand of my defender. It snapped through the net.

I fell into the flow of the game with no sense of self-concern and finished with 16 points, including five of eight three-point attempts. It was a big win, and the next night, back in the starting lineup against Western State, I made four three-pointers and scored 15 points. My crippling anxiety had become a distant memory, as if it had happened to somebody else. My fear morphed into excitement, and I felt alive.

After another solid game in a loss at Black Hills State I went cold against South Dakota Mines, making only 1 of 7 shots in a much-needed win. But my mind had become resilient. I felt satisfied that I'd continued to take shots with conviction even though I was missing. When self-doubt arose I was able to smile and let it pass, thanks to my practice on the meditation chair. I wasn't upset with my poor performance, and I was genuinely happy that we'd won the game.

In our next game, a win on the road, I hit five of seven shots, scored a team high of 15 points, and played a team high of 35 minutes. Toward the end of the game I told Coach during a dead ball to run our back pick play for me, because my defender had been losing track of me on the weak side. I was confident enough to know that finding an open three-pointer for me would be the team's best option. I was no longer an imposter.

4

We were clinging to a two-point lead in the final minutes of a crucial road game against Adams State. It had been three possessions since we'd scored, their crowd was loud, and we needed a basket to stop our opponents' momentum.

Our all-conference post player, Dexter Sienko, got the ball on the elbow and started his right-hand power move. Everything on the court seemed to slow down, and somehow I knew exactly what was about to happen. As my defender took a half step toward Dexter to help stop his drive, I shuffled a half step toward the baseline, giving me space to shoot. As Dexter's pass came hard at my chest my feet were already moving into my shot. I caught the ball in rhythm and felt myself rising up. I'd stopped making conscious decisions. It seemed as if I was watching myself shoot.

The ball released smoothly, and I watched its trajectory and rotation as it floated toward the hoop. I landed perfectly balanced, my follow-through holding firmly in the air. If that shot had bounced off the rim it would have surprised me as much as seeing the hoop and backboard transform into a waterfall. As the ball snapped through the net, my teammates on the bench behind me roared. Sprinting back on defense, I let loose a yell of joy. Later, watching the play on film, I saw our point guard Noah holding up three fingers and walking back on defense as soon as I caught the pass. He knew what was going to happen too.

Moments after making the shot I forgot about it, because it was time to concentrate on getting a defensive stop.

We won the game, and I finished with a career high of 20 points. It's my favorite memory among all my basketball experiences. Most of all, I was happy my family watched the game and were proud of me.

CHAPTER 20

FLOW

1

Barry Gillespie, an artist, woodworker and mindfulness teacher in Colorado, strikes me as someone reaping the benefits of decades of training in meditation. He seems truly joyful, peaceful, and comfortable in the world. I've sat a number of retreats with Barry, and he makes a useful distinction about mindfulness, describing mindfulness as a state of mind, rather than something we "do." It's being clearly aware without attachments or aversion. When we meditate we aren't practicing mindfulness, we're creating the causes and conditions that make mindfulness more likely to arise.

Mindfulness Coach George Mumford gives similar advice for finding "flow" on the court or the field. Instead of trying to manufacture positive states of mind, he recommends that we create the conditions that will make flow states likely, and then let it happen.

In his research, Michael Murphy asked countless athletes across sports about their experiences when they were "in the zone," and summarized his findings as follows: "Despite the many long years of instruction and practice that most athletes put in, they generally act spontaneously when they make outstanding plays. The conscious knowledge of correct and incorrect moves serves as kindling and logs to a fire, but in the white heat of the event they are burnt into nonexistence, as the reality of the flames takes over—flames originating in a source beyond conscious know-how, melding athlete, experience, and play into a single event."

Tim Gallwey comments on this seeming paradox in *The Inner Game of Tennis:*

> "But can one learn to play 'out of his mind' on purpose? How can you be consciously unconscious? It sounds like a contradiction in terms; yet this state can be achieved. Perhaps a better way to describe the player who is 'unconscious' is by saying that his mind is so concentrated, so focused, that it is still. It becomes one with what the body is doing, and the unconscious or automatic functions are working without interference from thoughts. The concentrated mind has no room for thinking how well the body is doing, much less of the how-to's of the doing. When a player is in this state, there is little to interfere with the full expression of his potential to perform, learn and enjoy."

As a senior, rather than trying to force myself into a positive state of mind, I focused on the preconditions that make flow states possible. I was consistent in my meditation practice, and when I showed up to the court I tried to bring absolute focus and intensity to the game, understanding that flow is the result of intense concentration.

I also understood that experience is constantly changing, and that these mind states would inevitably come and go. This helped me to not worry or get frustrated when my mind didn't feel its clearest on the court. Just as I'd practiced bringing my attention back to my breath thousands of times on the meditation chair, I repeatedly brought my attention back to the next rep, or the next play on the court. I repeatedly found myself in positive states of mind on the court, and my performance skyrocketed. As a senior I wasn't much bigger, faster, stronger or more coordinated than I'd been in previous years, but thanks to my mental improvements, I was an entirely different player.

2

German philosophy professor Eugen Herrigel taught in Japan in the 1920s. During his time there he studied Kyudo, the Japanese Art of Archery, with a Zen master. His experiences are related in his book, *Zen and the Art of Archery.*

He describes archery as a spiritual practice—an exercise in overcoming one's own ego. A primary goal of the teachings was to let go of expectations as to where an arrow would fly, and instead to focus entirely on the breath and one's own actions. For many years Herrigel wasn't permitted to shoot at a target, but instead a bale of hay, so as not to distract himself by worrying about the results. After some significant breakthroughs, the Master finally set up a target, but, again, Harrigel was told not to aim at the target when he shot, but rather to let the bow shoot itself.

One day Herrigel experienced a level of focus that he hadn't felt before, effortlessly releasing beautiful shots at the target. As a result his ego swelled with pride and satisfaction. His master noticed and told him the following:

"You know already that you should not grieve over bad shots; learn now not to rejoice over the good ones. You must free yourself from the buffetings of pleasure and pain, and learn to rise above them in easy equanimity, to rejoice as though not you but another had shot well. This, too, you must practice unceasingly—you cannot conceive how important it is."

In athletics we understand the importance of dealing with failure in a positive way, but what receives less attention in our athletic culture is our relationship with success. The two culprits responsible for loss of composure are attachment and aversion. Aversion to what we don't want, and our attachment to things we do want, cause our suffering.

Here's what Joseph Goldstein writes about the calm and composed mind in *Mindfulness*:

"The first way we experience the cool, restful quality of equanimity is in the peace and balance it brings to our daily lives. Each of us is touched by what are called 'the eight worldly vicissitudes.' These are the endlessly changing conditions of gain and loss, praise and blame, fame and disrepute, and pleasure and pain. When equanimity is developed, we ride these waves with balance and ease. Without it, we're tossed about by the waves, often crashing into the changing circumstances of our lives."

When reading this for the first time I was struck with how the things I considered "positive" are regarded as traps in the same way as the things I considered "negative." In Buddhism, gain, praise, fame, and pleasure are hindrances, just as their opposites are.

When a basketball team is on a scoring run, getting steals and pushing it out hard in transition, soaring in for dunks and splashing three-pointers, their behavior can be instructive. Teams that revel in success and fly too high in the good moments tend to be the same teams that come crashing down when things go wrong. The same players who were most exuberant during a good stretch will often shut down during a bad run, sometimes bickering with one another and committing costly fouls in their frustration. When great teams enjoy good stretches they don't lose their mental balance, and they come together instead of falling apart when they endure adversity.

As a senior, I had my first opportunity in years to deal with success. On the bus after big games I scrolled Twitter and glowed with pride as I saw my stat-line and highlights circulating on the internet. Former teammates and coaches I hadn't spoken to in years sent me congratulations. In January I was named athlete of the month at Regis, with my picture and statistics posted at the entrance of the gym.

I wanted to lap up this praise and validation, like a thirsty dog that's finally found water on a long, hot day. I was tempted to post highlights of myself on Instagram, along with a photo of my athlete of the month honors. But I'd been warned about this trap and understood that pride and self-aggrandizement in good times, and depression and anxiety in bad times, are two sides of the same dark coin, so when things finally started going my way I did my best to remain on an even keel.

3

Many athletes, coaches and motivational speakers know how important thoughts are in relation to performance. They know that when athletes feel calm and confident they tend to play well, and when they doubt themselves they'll likely play poorly. The question then becomes, how can we make ourselves feel calm and confident more often? The standard American sports culture answer is to think positively. I tried to apply this advice by repeating the following affirmations to myself before games and even on the court:

"You're going to make your next shot."

"You're a great shooter."

"You're going to make the all-conference team."

And even this: "You're the best, toughest motherfucker on the court."

Sometimes it worked temporarily, but the confidence I'd manufactured usually disappeared within a few moments. Positive thinking or "self-talk" addressed my surface level feelings, but not the core of my mind. Tim Gallwey dealt with this issue in *The Inner Game of Tennis*:

"Before finishing with the subject of the judgmental mind, something needs to be said about 'positive thinking.' The 'bad' effects of negative thinking are frequently discussed these days. Books and articles advise readers to replace negative thinking with positive thinking. People are advised to stop telling themselves they are ugly, uncoordinated, unhappy or whatever, and to repeat to themselves that they are attractive, well coordinated and happy. The substitution of a kind of 'positive hypnotism' for a previous habit of 'negative hypnotism' may appear at least to have short-range benefits, but I have always found that the honeymoon ends all too soon."

No matter how hard I tried to think positively, my confidence was still tied to my performance. This positive self-talk might work for some, but for me it was counterproductive. The language of the lines above is married to the stories we tell ourselves about our reputations, and they often subtly reinforce the insecurities we're trying to escape. When I was truly confident as a senior, I felt no inclination to repeat these phrases to myself. I knew I was an excellent shooter, and I didn't have to convince myself.

4

If you aren't truly confident in yourself, how do you cultivate such confidence? In my experience it comes from focusing on the present moment, nonjudgmental awareness, an attitude of courage and bravery, and trusting that things will get better if you stay the course. Paying attention to the feelings of insecurity, anxiety, and stress works better than pushing them away.

Sustainable confidence can be developed through mental training, not temporarily tricking the mind into positive states. The visualization practices that my therapist taught me were a productive kind of "positive thinking." When you drop down a level and use imagery, you're visualizing the *experience* of proper and successful movements on the court or the field. The difference is important: instead of telling yourself you're going to make your next shot, you see and feel yourself shooting with proper balance and rhythm, and a smooth release with proper lift and arc on your shot.

When you envision yourself playing, you aren't caught in thoughts and stories about your statistics, or your perceived standing or status on the team, or the concepts of "good" and "bad" play. You're connecting with the actual experience. With training, the skill of visualization improves over time. By the time I was a senior, I'd really gotten the hang of it. I could see myself knocking down shots from all over the court, and I could visualize plays being run for me, watch them unfold, and see and feel myself knocking down big shots.

To be clear, these were not fantasies about glorious performances, they were simple and successful repetitions. Nobody really knows for sure why visualization works. Strange data has come back from various studies showing that those who visualize themselves weightlifting actually grow stronger. The same is true for free-throw shooting. When compared with a control group, those who visualize themselves making free throws show significant improvements. Whether or not this is some version of the placebo effect, it works.

5

"And yet as a coach, I know that being fixated on winning (or more likely, not losing) is counterproductive, especially when it causes you to lose control of your emotions. What's more, obsessing about winning is a loser's game: The most we can hope for is to create the best possible conditions for success, then let go of the outcome. The ride is a lot more fun that way."

- Phil Jackson

On the meditation chair we practice the art of non-preferential awareness. Rather than constantly seeking comfort, a meditator sits still and surrenders to experience. A meditator pays close attention to experience without trying to change or improve it, and observes how pleasant and unpleasant sensations, emotions, and moods arise and pass away. The goal is to understand experiences without reacting to them. This practice, and its underlying philosophy, can be applied and tested in athletic competition.

Instead of fixating on winning and playing well individually, we can bring full effort, energy, and awareness to the game, and let it unfold as it will. This might seem paradoxical, but letting go of rigid expectations can be liberating, and lead to greater success.

While developing a composed mind free from aversion and attachment is challenging, it's the only way to escape a mental treadmill. Instead of constantly trying to manipulate experiences and outcomes, we can simply surrender to the inevitable and uncontrollable ups and downs of sports and life, and stay in touch with the ever-present inevitability of constant change. Clear awareness of experience is intrinsically pleasant, and creates a sustainable happiness. Constant attempts to manipulate experience don't often lead to the desired results. And even when we get exactly what we want, we don't stay happy all that long.

What I often get when I recommend impartiality to experience is a fear that it might be de-motivating and lead to apathy. But equanimity shouldn't be confused with detachment. The goal is to care more about mental clarity, engagement, and focus on the task at hand than about what the result will be—in other words, to control no more or less than what you can actually control. As Goldstein puts it, "We can do what we do with full commitment, but the outcome is often beyond our control. When we act without attachment to the outcome, then our minds remain peaceful no matter how things unfold." Here is Phil Jackson's recommendation to his players: "Approach the game with no preset agendas and you'll probably come away surprised at your overall efforts."

6

I've described how a big moment in a big baseball game transformed my attitude toward my friend. When he hit his home run to give us the lead late in a playoff game, his success and happiness felt like it was my own. My envy and the tension I generally felt toward him disappeared.

Nearly all of us pay lip service to wanting others to be happy. But we also gauge our perceived status and compare it to the status of others. When our good friend enjoys some success we often feel envious. Some of us are satisfied with pretending to be happy for our friends and teammates when they play well, while we keep a dark secret to ourselves.

A certain level of competition between teammates is a positive sign of a healthy program. Players should want to contribute to the tribe, and want to improve their own situations. The battles for playing time, a bigger role, and starting positions can result in growth for everyone involved, which in turn creates a stronger team. Any player perfectly happy to sit on the bench, like I was as a college sophomore, isn't in the right mental state. As mentioned earlier, it's not always beneficial to avoid conflict with teammates or anyone else.

But competition between teammates becomes corrosive when it translates into schadenfreude for teammates' failures. I consider the secret satisfaction I took in seeing my friends miss a shot or strike out as the most shameful moments of my athletic life. The offseason and preseason are appropriate times to cultivate competition between teammates and friends, but when the season starts the competition has to be concentrated against other teams. Roles change through the course of a season, and competition between teammates inevitably persists, but an athlete wishing failure on his friends is definitely missing the central point.

7

The more we pay attention to our own minds, the more we collide head-on with the unflattering thoughts that used to capture our minds without us noticing. It can be painful to confront our dark intentions toward others, but noticing negative thoughts without being identified with them is how we can begin to change.

As a senior, I recognized my harmful attitudes and did my best to pay attention to them, and then recommit to what I wanted—to wish the best for friends and teammates, and to care more about how we're playing as a team than my own statline. I discovered that with practice this attitude can be cultivated even in ordinary practices and games. It doesn't take a pressure-packed moment with huge implications to discover a healthier viewpoint.

Consider a situation in which all athletes sometimes find themselves—you play poorly but your team wins.

Or, to make the situation even more difficult, your back-up, who's been competing with you for your starting position, played well and made a huge contribution down the stretch. After the game, the team, coaching staff, and fans are elated. Hopefully you're happy that you won the game, but your mind is probably clouded with thoughts about your own poor performance, limiting your ability to enjoy the moment. "What's my scoring average now? What if my backup starts instead of me in the next game, or sometime later in the season?" Thoughts like these can put an athlete into a downward mental spiral resulting in a loss of respect from teammates.

In my third-to-last game of my senior season I shot 1-7 from the three-point line and finished with four points in a big road win that kept our playoff hopes alive. I'd also struggled on defense, when I was taken advantage of in the post by a bigger, stronger guard, which resulted in me getting benched during the final minutes. As I jogged back to the locker room, the awful thoughts rushed in: "I've shot so well all year, what if I go cold now and finish under 40% from the three-point line? What if I get yanked from the starting lineup at the end of the season?" But instead of surrendering to the useless habit of fixating on the worst-case scenario, I understood these thoughts and smiled to myself at their absurdity, and then celebrated with teammates, laughing and dancing to rap music in the locker room. This game turned out to be the last win of our season and the last win of my career, and I'm thankful not to have spoiled it for myself, or anyone else, with a selfish attitude.

Controlling thoughts and emotions isn't as easy as it sounds, so what should a player do who feels bad after a win? Even if it comes off as somewhat insincere, I think it's still best to summon some enthusiasm and excitement, not in an attempt to fool yourself or others, but as a way to cultivate the better part of yourself. In these moments you're communicating to your teammates (and to yourself) that even though you're unhappy with your own performance, you're happy that you won the game.

CHAPTER 21

CONNECTION

1

After Christmas break I averaged 27 minutes per game and nearly 12 points on 45% shooting from both the field and three-point line. I made shots from well beyond the three-point line, which spread the floor and created space for our offense to function more effectively.

My coaches put me in a position to succeed by simplifying my role and encouraging me to concentrate on what I was good at. As a senior I made 73 shots, 70 of them threes—96% of my made field goals. During a season in which I didn't find my confidence until after Christmas break, my made three-pointers were the fourth most in school history. By season's end defenders were sprinting at me whenever I caught a pass, daring me to put the ball on the floor. In previous years I'd often been overwhelmed by bigger, more athletic defenders in the paint. As a senior my coaches worked with me on pump faking to get my defender to fly by, establishing room for me to launch a three anyway.

They encouraged me to shoot from deep, far beyond the three-point line, and had me practice extra-long shots daily, something that would have gotten me yelled at by my former coach. They helped me improve my defensive skills. I was still a liability on defense, but I did well enough within their system to stay on the court. With below average foot speed, I relied on my mind to help me gain an extra half step. I played defense hard, but with a soft, precise focus similar to what I experienced while meditating. I was usually able to react quickly and get myself to where I needed to be.

Beyond personal success, I was connecting as I never had before with the beauty of basketball and the excitement of competition. I routinely found myself in flow states, where everything superfluous dropped away, and only the game remained. I loved my teammates and going into battle with them. I wanted to play well, but I *truly* cared mostly about winning with the team playing well. I loved my coaches and I fought for them during every practice and game.

We played in some intense games down the stretch, fighting for the final conference playoff spot. I enjoyed the thrill and uncertainty of our collective goal. We fell out of contention in our final week, but playing in close, meaningful games produced the best athletic moments of my life.

I'd enjoyed much greater personal success in high school when I was usually the best player on the court, and one of the best on the baseball field as we chased state championships. In comparison, my final college season was ordinary—I was the fifth best player on a competitive team—but I connected with what matters.

This proved to me that state of mind has more to do with satisfaction than outward circumstances. As a high school star I was generally dissatisfied, rarely taking time to appreciate my good fortune. Instead, I often found things to complain about, and was constantly looking ahead toward future goals.

Throughout my final college season I knew I wouldn't be playing professionally, so I let myself enjoy each practice and game. I didn't worry about it ending or wish it away. I remained in the present, grateful for everything I had. I never expected everything to work out perfectly. I had bad games and was criticized by my coach. I still dreaded tedious ball handling drills and exhausting workouts in the weight room. There were days when I watched the clock, looking forward to the end of practice. But I enjoyed a much-improved relationship with basketball. My final season wasn't a stepping stone toward some future, greater goal, it was what I had and what I could do.

2

In our next-to-last game we lost to Colorado Mesa, eliminating us from playoff contention, leaving one remaining game in my athletic career.

In all my years playing sports growing up, I never thought about the fact that someday I'd lace up my sneakers before a game for the last time. There would be adult leagues, but I'd never compete within the context of a long season, sharing the struggle and bonding with my teammates and friends. A shared sentiment among athletes is that the last game is the death of an athletic life.

My final game in high school had gone poorly. I was so affected by melodramatic nostalgia that I didn't enjoy it and didn't play well. Before my final college game I felt peaceful nostalgia that blended pleasantly with gratitude for a final opportunity to play the game I loved. As I'd done all year long, I did my pregame meditation, set my intentions, drank my coffee, and studied the scouting report. I didn't try to manufacture emotion during my normal pregame shooting and ball handling routines.

There were moments when I lost track of the fact that this was my last game. I was doing my best to help us win. At times I noticed how my feet felt on the court, how the ball felt when I caught a pass, and details of the panoramic view of the court as I sprinted up and down the floor. I paid attention to the beauty and synergy of basketball, and the conflict between chaos (defense) and order (offense) on every possession.

During a timeout late in the game I sat on the bench, breathing hard and sweating. I took a water cup from the athletic trainer's assistant. While waiting for Coach to address us, I suddenly and unexpectedly connected with the fact that there were players on the other team who were also playing in their final games, and that their own athletic journeys were no less valuable than mine. I thought about the thousands of athletes across America and around the world that were also playing final games, and how all of them had experienced struggles and triumphs, anxiety and joy. Finally I thought about the millions of children who play and compete. And I felt the same love for my opponents that I did for my teammates and coaches, because they were part of the beauty and uncertainty of my final game. Without a chance of losing, what would winning mean? What is success without the chance of failure? Then I heard the whiteboard drop to the floor, snapping my attention back toward Coach. I paid attention to his instructions on changing our ball screen coverages.

I finished the game with 10 points, making 3 of 6 three-pointers, and 1 of 2 free throws. We mounted a comeback but fell short in the end, and lost by seven. In the locker room afterward I removed my shoes and ankle tape for the last time. Unlike the end of many seasons before, when I felt like I was *supposed* to be emotional, I was quiet and calm. After Coach thanked the seniors, we broke our final huddle and hugged each other and expressed our love.

When I hugged my best friend Dylan, I felt the weight of our shared history together: all the miserable morning practices, the repressed laugh attacks in the locker room, the drunken antics at parties, the hangovers, the great games, the shooting slumps. I appreciated everything, and I felt myself wanting to cry. Then, when I hugged my head coach, who'd saved my love for sports, I did cry.

Chapter 22

MENTAL HEALTH IN SPORTS

1

According to the National Institute of Mental Health, nearly one in five adults and one in three adolescent children suffer from some form of anxiety disorder. College students, athletes among them, are becoming more anxious and depressed all the time. A 2016 report by the Center for Collegiate Mental Health, using data from 139 colleges, found that by the 2015-2016 school year, *half* of all students surveyed reported having attended counseling for mental health concerns.

Some of the disturbing upticks we're seeing in depression and anxiety data are the result of more people seeking help and discussing their problems openly. But we're also seeing upward trends in self-harm and suicide amongst adolescents and young adults, indicating that there is indeed a problem with mental health that's getting worse.

There are people suffering from truly awful mental health problems, like schizophrenia, bipolar disorder, post traumatic stress disorder, etc. People with these problems have often suffered unbearable traumas and tragedies, sometimes in childhood. The focus of this chapter is not on these deeper problems, but instead concentrates on athletes who are dealing with issues similar to those I dealt with. My objective is to help struggling athletes better understand their issues and hopefully recover.

2

When I showed up at Regis I was unprepared to play in the Rocky Mountain Athletic Conference. I was overwhelmed by the pace of the game, and the athleticism of my opponents. It's clear to me in hindsight that I would have benefitted from spending a year as a red shirt, or riding the bench, as I grew accustomed to the intensity of college basketball.

I also had limited experience with tough coaching. The success and relative lack of adversity I experienced in high school left me completely unprepared for Coach Porter, who was fiercely demanding, and didn't hold back in his criticisms of his players. But even as it happened I knew that blaming my issues on my head coach wasn't fair. Most of my teammates were unhappy too, and many were more fiercely criticized than I was, but, as far as I knew, none were staving off anxiety attacks before practice, or having trouble breathing at the free throw line. I've also come to understand that while my basketball struggles were at the core of my issues with anxiety, I also contend with anxieties that have nothing to do with sports. So why was I so messed up?

Were my issues the result of some childhood trauma? Not that I can remember. I had a loving and supportive family, and enjoyed a relatively healthy childhood.

Was it a genetically influenced medical condition—a chemical imbalance in the brain? There's anxiety and addiction in my family tree, which would support such a conclusion.

Were my problems the result of my flawed life philosophy, my poor habits and behaviors? This makes sense, because changing my outlook, habits, and behaviors helped me. But this doesn't help everyone.

Or were my issues a spiritual problem? I was a hardened materialist without any form of spirituality at the time, so that could be true.

Or perhaps my problems were the result of the culture I lived in. This seems reasonable, as I'd adopted a hyper self-critical attitude common in modern athletics, and tried to fight and struggle my way toward future success. I was desperate to live up to the expectations set by my scholarship and to please the coaching staff, which led me to put immense pressure on myself to perform.

More generally, modern youth culture consists largely of distraction and pleasure seeking, looking at screens instead of trees and rivers, craving followers and likes, swiping dating apps and watching porn, and eating and drinking junk. How could that not lead to anxiety and depression?

Scott Stossel, in his *Atlantic* article "Surviving Anxiety," describes his own lifelong struggles with anxiety disorders. He writes the following:

> "The truth is that anxiety is at once a function of biology and philosophy, body and mind, instinct and reason, personality and culture. Even as anxiety is experienced at a spiritual and psychological level, it is scientifically measurable at the molecular level and the physiological level. It is produced by nature and it is produced by nurture. It's a psychological phenomenon and a sociological phenomenon. In computer terms, it's both a hardware problem (I'm wired badly) and a software problem (I run

faulty logic programs that make me think anxious thoughts). The origins of a temperament are many-faceted; emotional dispositions that seem to have a simple, single source—a bad gene, say, or a childhood trauma—may not."

3

Athletes are at a mental health advantage in some respects. In an isolated and fragmented modern world, being on a sports team offers a sense of collective purpose, a shared sense of struggle, a tribe. This is one of the most positive things about being a team sport athlete. For most sports, weight lifting and physical exercise are built into the athletic experience, which certainly helps with issues of mental health. Successful athletes are often popular in school, and enjoy a sense of self confidence that's based on athletic success.

But athletes are disadvantaged in other ways. The stress and pressure placed on modern young athletes, either by overzealous parents, or by society, or in my case, by one's own self, can be overpowering. Promising youth athletes feel the pressure to play on the most prestigious travel teams, and spend much of their childhood in pressure packed athletic events. Given the nature of our college education system, which leaves so many people strapped with lifelong debt and financial hardship, an athletic scholarship can be a life changing accomplishment for both an athlete and her family. This leads many high school athletes and their families to become obsessed with athletic improvement and exposure to college scouts, sometimes leading to both physical and mental burnout, and the evaporation of any joy in playing sports.

College athletes, especially those who take academics seriously, are asked to maintain absurd schedules. The pressure to perform both athletically and academically, paired with the healthy desire to enjoy a social life, can overwhelm an athlete who's also learning how to live away from home for the first time.

Underperforming athletes are at especially high risk for mental health issues, as the blessings mentioned above can become points of misery. Committed athletes often build their identities around athletic success, and don't cultivate interests outside of sports. When they stop having success, they lose what they'd been relying on for self confidence and meaning in life.

All of us seek connection, and we want to be useful to our tribe members. Struggling, underperforming athletes live with constant guilt for not contributing enough. I suspect that this is why failing athletes often suffer mental health problems. When an underperforming athlete becomes anxious and depressed, it leads to further diminished performance, which leads to more anxiety, and so on. Escaping this negative spiral is bound to be difficult.

4

"Athletes don't get help for depression or mental health issues because they can't even admit that it's an issue. That's fundamentally at odds with what it means to be a competitor."

- Olympic figure skater Sasha Cohen

What further complicates the situation for athletes is the fact that mental toughness is not only an advantage in competition, but perhaps the most helpful quality an athlete can have. The heroes of each generation are athletes who demonstrate what Ernest Hemingway defined as the most important human virtue: "grace under pressure."

Professional athletes who melt under pressure in their biggest moments can be ridiculed by fans, sports journalists, and commentators. Athletes who succeed under pressure are always praised and admired, so it makes complete sense that young athletes see their mental issues as failings that should be hidden from others. My best friend in college knew I was having a tough sophomore season, but had no idea how bad things were, because I kept my problems to myself. WNBA guard Katie Lou Samuelson, who wrote in an ESPN article about her struggles with anxiety and depression, did the same thing:

> "I was really effective at hiding it; my friends and my family, they had no idea. I kept everything to myself. That's one of my issues, too: I didn't want anyone to feel I was burdening them or making excuses."

In an HBO documentary titled *The Weight of Gold,* many Olympic athletes describe their issues with mental health. Olympic superstar Michael Phelps is featured in the production, and he thinks athletes resist seeking help because of the "conviction that we can make ourselves unbeatable if we just work at it. Our belief that there's no way that *we* should need help. Our fear that we'll become weak if we show any vulnerability."

A turning point for sports and mental health issues occurred when star power forward Kevin Love posted his 2018 article *Everyone is Going Through Something*, where he wrote in detail about leaving an NBA game due to a panic attack. Love writes:

> "Growing up, you figure out really quickly how a boy is supposed to act. You learn what it takes to 'be a man.' It's like a playbook: Be strong. Don't talk about your feelings. Get through it on your own. So for 29 years of my life, I followed that playbook. And look, I'm probably not telling you anything new here. These values about men and toughness are so ordinary that they're everywhere ... and invisible at the same time, surrounding us like air or water. They're a lot like depression or anxiety in that way."

Since Love, many more athletes have opened up about their mental health issues. Demar DeRozan, all-star guard for the San Antonio Spurs, described his struggles with depression since his childhood. Philadelphia Eagles right guard Brandon Brooks missed an NFL game due to anxiety induced vomiting, and said he'd been struggling with overwhelming anxiety throughout his career. More recently, America's (and the world's) premier female gymnast, Simone Biles, dropped out of an event at the Tokyo Olympics because, as she explained, she was experiencing extreme anxiety—physically shaking before the event and worried that she'd get injured if she tried to perform.

5

It's necessary to note that anxiety is an inevitable part of the athletic experience, and that some degree of it is actually healthy. Any athlete who feels no "jitters" before a game probably isn't in the right mental state for peak performance. But an athlete experiencing so much anxiety that it inhibits performance and causes dread outside of sport is an athlete with a very serious problem.

For those dealing with an unhealthy level of anxiety and/or depression, my first recommendation is to seek professional help. If you have access to a therapist or a sports psychologist, and you need help, deciding to make an appointment can be the best decision you've ever made. Seeking necessary help isn't a failure, but might well be the act of courage that both saves your athletic career and favorably alters the course of your life.

I'd also recommend, assuming you have the resources, that you choose your therapist carefully. Since my first therapist changed my life I've seen other professionals, and I've realized that, as in any other profession, there's a spectrum of talent and competency. Some of the therapists have been wise, compassionate, and effective. Others have seemed more troubled than I was, and only made things worse. I've met some clearly troubled individuals in my social life who are also therapists. One can jump through the hoops of getting the relevant degrees in psychology without gaining the wisdom or skill to be effective.

If you don't feel a positive chemistry with your first choice, look elsewhere. This doesn't mean therapy should be fun, or always make you feel good. Therapy can be tough, and whoever you work with will inevitably be another flawed, imperfect human being, but you have to trust and respect the person you're opening up to.

I was fortunate to collide with a very skilled therapist, and I'm grateful to her for helping me grow strong enough to face my anxiety head-on. She didn't try to convince me that somehow everything would eventually be fine just as it was, or allow me to use anxiety as an excuse for all my problems. She helped me realize that I shouldn't feel ashamed of my anxiety, and that I could deal with it, even if it never went away. Through meditation, I practiced a new relationship to the experience of anxiety (more on this in the next chapter). Instead of trying to push the feeling away, I let it engulf me, and in doing so discovered that anxiety lost its power.

I was dealing with a phobia about shooting in front of my coaches and teammates. In the summer after my awful season, my therapist helped me expose myself to situations that brought on the anxiety, and practice dealing with them. She helped me understand my habit of "catastrophizing"—irrationally viewing unpleasant incidents (like badly missing a free throw) as events that would ruin my life.

We worked on my habits—sleep, diet, mindfulness, my relationship to alcohol and partying, and my overuse of my phone and social media.

We also talked about my issues, and understanding where my fears were located helped me re-frame them. I read transformative books, which armed me with new forms of wisdom and resilience.

Through all of this, and through the good luck of having supportive family and friends and a new and excellent head coach as a senior, I slowly recovered, and my mind has become much stronger than it ever was before the collapse.

6

The traditional way of viewing anxiety as something soft, an embarrassment that should be hidden from others, is clearly unhealthy, and, finally, the stigma has begun to lose its power. The courage of professional athletes to open up about their issues has made space for young athletes to reflect on their own mental health. But once the stigma breaks, we need to be careful, both individually and collectively, not to end up at an opposite extreme, which would include openly broadcasting anxiety to others, and using it as an excuse.

In my sessions with Libby from YoMind, she discovered my tendency to label myself as someone with anxiety. She often heard me say, "I'm an anxious person" or "I have anxiety issues." What she made clear to me was that when I said these things, my brain was listening.

Libby defined this as a process of reification. Repeating "I have anxiety issues" established my identity as an anxious person, which was not only counterproductive, but also untrue. She helped me realize that, like almost everyone, sometimes I experienced anxiety and sometimes I didn't. Perhaps I felt negative emotions more often than some others, but that didn't define me as an anxious person through and through. When I stopped telling myself and others that I had anxiety, I experienced a significant, positive change.

It can be effective to treat serious subjects with humor, as when *South Park* commented on the new, fashionable habit of using anxiety as a counterproductive excuse to retreat from life. Cartman is diagnosed with anxiety by his therapist, and to remedy his problem he purchases a cardboard box ironically called a "Buddha Box" that rests over his head, allowing him to scroll his phone while shutting out the rest of the world. When his school principal asks him what he's doing, he replies, "I'm letting go of stress and being calm like the Buddha." Later, he holds up the line at the waterpark and sits on Kyle's towel with the Buddha box over his head while scrolling his phone. Kyle, fed up with Cartman, angrily flips the box off his head and yells, "Get off my towel!"

"Goddammit!" Catman answers. "I seriously can't get a minute of peace! Why is it that people who don't have a Buddha Box are always flipping Buddha Boxes off the heads of people with anxiety?"

Then Kyle gets to the point: "I've got news for you, Cartman, everyone has anxiety! Everyone gets nervous! Everyone gets afraid of being around people! Everyone has feelings they'd rather stay home alone! And do you know what they do? They get over it, and they stop being a piece of shit!"

Regarding anxiety as a disease that's completely out of the control of the person suffering it can give short term relief to the sufferer. For example, social anxiety can be used as an excuse to stay home and not go to the party. But this identity of victimhood can ultimately prevent people from making the necessary changes that would help them recover, or at least improve their long term situations.

Anxious athletes shouldn't feel ashamed of their anxieties, but should want to recover and overcome them, or learn to both play and live with them.

Had I been taught to avoid the things that made me afraid, I'd have been stuck where I was forever—anxious and depressed. Had I been encouraged to broadcast my anxiety to others, anxiety would have remained an integral part of my identity. So, while I'm happy to see the traditional stigmas surrounding mental health in sports losing their strength, there should always be something admirable about quiet courage and pushing ahead despite anxiety and fear.

7

"Indeed, when you go through mood swings, you now have to justify why you are not on some medication. There may be a few good reasons to be on medication, in severely pathological cases, but my mood, my sadness, my bouts of anxiety, are a second source of intelligence—perhaps even the first source."

- Nassim Taleb in Antifragile

I'm not a pharmacologist, and I have no experience in clinical research. My attitude towards medication is the result of my own experience, paired with my reading and research. What I write below doesn't apply to those suffering from the truly awful and unmanageable mental health issues that I listed to begin the chapter. But for athletes who are dealing with debilitating performance anxiety and/or struggling with depression, yet are still functioning relatively well as people, I recommend trying other solutions before resorting to anti-anxiety medication or antidepressants.

It's my understanding that medication for anxiety is not as effective as many people tend to think, especially over long periods of time. In "Surviving Anxiety," Scott Stossel writes that "While lots of people will testify that drugs have helped them, lots of other people will testify (and often do, in court filings and before Congress) that medication has ruined their lives." He points out that psychiatrists' favorite drugs are often no more effective than sugar pills regarding long term improvement, and that many users experience devastating side effects and withdrawal symptoms.

I agree with Stossel that my issues with anxiety are a combination of many factors (psychological, philosophical, behavioral, spiritual, and chemical), and I worry that artificially numbing my emotional pain might prevent me from making helpful alterations to my philosophies, relationships, and behaviors.

That's why I recommend that athletes with experiences similar to mine be wary of anti-anxiety medications or antidepressants, and instead focus on other behavioral changes: committing to a mental training and meditation regimen; seriously connecting with deep and sincerely held values or faith; staying connected with people who care about you; becoming more disciplined with sleep and diet; deleting social media accounts; reducing alcohol and/or pot consumption; getting off unprescribed adderall; getting out of toxic relationships; becoming less obsessed with academic perfection; creating more time for leisure in daily life; making an effort to be kinder and more compassionate to others; spending more time outside in the sun, etc. And one way or another, athletes dealing with performance anxiety need to confront their sports-specific fears.

8

"The pro-psychedelic position is an anti-drug position."

- Terrance McKenna

I need to add that early evidence coming back from therapy with psychedelic drugs is very encouraging—specifically with psilocybin, the psychoactive compound in "magic mushrooms." Solid evidence concludes that just one or two sessions with psilocybin, taken with a trained guide, yield far better results than any other medication currently available. What's especially noteworthy is that those who report having a "spiritual" psilocybin experience are very likely to report significant and long-term relief from depression and anxiety symptoms, PTSD, alcoholism, nicotine addiction, and eating disorders.

Psychedelic drugs are commonly and mistakenly lumped together with truly destructive drugs such as heroin and cocaine. While psychedelics can be disrespected and misused, they're relatively non-toxic and are not addictive.

In November, 2020, HBO's *Real Sports* documented three athletes suffering from chronic traumatic encephalopathy (CTE). After two-time Stanley Cup champion Daniel Carcillo retired from the NHL, he suffered from ongoing light sensitivity, slurred speech, headaches, head pressure, concentration issues, short and long-term memory loss, and debilitating depression and anxiety. He'd begun planning his suicide before making a final attempt at improvement by flying to Peru to participate in a shamanistic ceremony during which he took ayahuasca—a potent psychedelic that's illegal in much of the world. He reported a long, difficult "trip" wherein he was "visited" by his deceased grandparents. After the trip his CTE symptoms disappeared. Many months later his wife reported he'd become the loving husband and father she'd married.

To some, this may sound fantastical, but these immediate transformations are actually commonplace. Kerry Rhodes, an elite safety in the NFL for eight years, reported having been cured of CTE-related symptoms after his ayahuasca ceremony.

Retired UFC fighter Ian McCall, addicted to painkillers and drinking 20 beers a day, said he'd chosen a particular beam in his house to hang himself from. Six months after a major dose of psilocybin, he still hadn't had any alcohol or painkillers and felt like a brand new person.

My own limited experience confirms what these examples suggest, and I sometimes wonder whether an adequate dose of psilocybin mushrooms, administered by a competent guide in a therapeutic setting, would have helped me get back on track during my sophomore season. I'm certain it would have done far more good than the alcohol I drank every weekend.

Young athletes need to understand that there's a big difference between dropping acid at a music festival and taking a deliberate psychedelic journey in a safe setting with drugs that have been tested for purity. These drugs are powerful and need to be respected as such. I write this a few weeks after my home state of Oregon passed ground-breaking legislation making psilocybin therapy with a trained and accredited guide legal. It's probable that in the not too distant future, psychedelic therapies will help many suffering people, with athletes among them.

CHAPTER 23

THE MEDICINE OF PRACTICE

1

In *Altered Traits,* Dan Goleman and Richard Davidson conclude that consistent practice in mindfulness-based meditation leads to a decrease in depression and anxiety as effectively as the best medication, but without any side effects. Besides recent scientific claims, thousands of years of testimony that spans many cultures and religions suggest that the practice can transform the mind in positive and durable ways. It's my experience that practicing clear concentration and non-judgmental awareness off the court helped me find the flow states on the court that took my game to new levels.

While I wouldn't wish the misery I suffered early in my college basketball career on anyone, in some ways I'm thankful for it. My depression and anxiety drew me to meditation and an interest in understanding my own mind. Because the mental aspects of sport are far more difficult to define and analyze than the physical aspects, too many athletes try to convince themselves that they can cultivate a desired state of mind simply by wanting it, or telling themselves they want it. Or they believe that they can attain a state of mind by thinking and talking about it, convincing themselves that when the game starts what they need will be there. But for those of us struggling with self-doubt, thinking our way into a positive mental state isn't sustainable.

Examine this common athletic advice: "Control what you can control, and don't worry about the rest." This seems sensible, but how can it be done? How do you stop worrying about things you can't control? You can tell yourself every day or two, or every hour or two, that you should do it, but, if you're struggling with anxiety, any confidence acquired that way will likely evaporate within minutes. Coaches don't tell their players to "jump higher" or to "be stronger." Instead, they help them train so that they can gradually improve their athleticism.

As with any physical attribute we can name—endurance, strength, coordination—each of us possesses a spectrum of raw talent, or potential. A few are born with exceptional leaping ability while others can barely get off the ground. Likewise, some of us have an innate capacity to focus clearly on a task at hand, while others have minds easily distracted by thoughts and fears, making it difficult to concentrate.

Those of us who battle anxiety and self-doubt have work to do in order to achieve mental toughness, just as someone who's overweight has work to do to make the soccer team. We can't tell ourselves to be fit, and then sit back and wait for it to happen.

Athletic competition is its own kind of mental training for life at large. Athletes learn how to deal with adversity, stress and pressure. They learn how to show up and give energy and effort even when they don't feel like it. They learn the importance of individual sacrifice for the sake of collective success. They learn how to respond to criticism. Many former athletes thrive in the job market because the stress and pressure they face in an office pale in comparison to what they faced as athletes. But not all athletes are born with minds that can deal successfully with pressure, so if sports are mental training for life at large, how does an athlete mentally train for sports?

The good news is that as with physical skills and traits, mental capabilities can be improved through disciplined practice. In his *Waking Up* app, Sam Harris draws a useful comparison between physical and mental training. He points out that not very long ago people who dedicated themselves to physical training and exercise were thought to be strange and eccentric. It was culturally weird behavior, with the unfortunate result that nearly everyone missed out on the benefits it offered. Harris argues that there is still a sizable cultural blind spot regarding mental training: "There are people who lose 100 pounds and become competitive tri-athletes. However rare those extreme transformations are, we know that they're possible, and the rest of us pursue our own efforts at physical self-improvement on that same landscape of possibility." He goes on to make the important point that most of us remain unaware that it's possible to transform our minds in a similar way.

Obviously, meditating and training the mind alone won't make anyone a great athlete. The skills specific to our sports are an indispensable component. But for some of us, mental limitations set a glass ceiling, drastically inhibiting our physical skills in competition. To reap the benefits of the work we put in on our skills, strength, and endurance, we have to work on mental skills so that we can surpass limitations set by our minds. Athletes who don't struggle with anxiety can benefit from this advice as well. At the upper levels of sport, where every competitor is extremely talented, it's usually a mental or "spiritual" edge that separates the truly special players from everyone else. In *The Last Dance*, a documentary about Michael Jordan's final season with the Bulls, author Mark Vancil said the following:

> "Most people live in fear because we project the past into the future. Micheal's a mystic—he was never anywhere else. His gift was not that he could jump high, run fast, and shoot a basketball. His gift was that he was completely present, and that was the separator."

2

My mental training eventually allowed me to reach the first rung on the ladder out of darkness. Not running from my problems produced enough mental space for me to start making better decisions, which gradually compounded. I soon became mindful enough to realize that neither trying to sleep all day nor drinking all weekend made any sense. I started eating better food and getting more sleep, and these decisions allowed me to gain some mental clarity.

Ever since I was a child I've had the tendency to overthink and overanalyze, and my mind can spin in unending loops. I tried to think my way out of my problems by imagining the worst possible case scenario, and then wondering what things would look like when that occurred. The practice of meditation allowed me to stop warring against my own mind. Sitting in silence and following the breath yields wisdom that new information, incessant thinking, and rumination cannot. Slowly, my practice shifted from just a way to feel better and get back to "normal," to a way to optimize performance, and then to a way to connect with the beauty of sports and life.

Meditation creates a low-stress, low-pressure environment where we can practice helpful mental skills over and over again. While sitting and attempting to meditate, countless distractions arise. We're challenged by feelings of being tired, bored, restless, and impatient. Each time we recognize these states of mind, and bring our concentration back to the object of awareness, like the breath, our minds grow slightly stronger.

3

Athletes respond in many different ways to criticism and conflict. When getting criticized or yelled at by our coach, some of my teammates reflexively blamed the coach for singling them out and being unfair. These teammates also had a false, if somewhat useful, perception of their own talents and abilities. When they played poorly they often blamed the referees, the system, or their teammates for not sharing the ball. While these teammates had their own issues, like occasional selfishness and arrogance, they seldom struggled with anxiety or issues of confidence. But players like me have the opposite impulse—I was always keenly aware of my limitations as a player. Being yelled at by my coach made me feel horrible, and I wanted desperately to do better and make him happy. I tried to maintain peace and avoid conflict with teammates and friends. This definitely contributed to my anxiety on the court, and I know other players with the same temperament who had similar struggles.

I imagine this same dynamic applies to famous athletes who deal with criticisms from the media, and that players with my kind of temperament take it especially hard.

I know my mental training made me more comfortable with conflict, which made me a better player and a more complete person. As my practice developed, criticism from my coach no longer made me shut down as a player. I could absorb what I thought was true and deflect what I thought was unfair. Meditation also helped me stand up to conflict, and not back down from challenges from teammates in practice and opponents in games. I was able to notice the tension that conflict produces and let it linger, rather than trying to alleviate it as quickly as I could.

I think players like me—overthinkers prone to self doubt—can benefit from being more assertive both on the court and off. Meditation practice helps us recognize our tendency to keep the peace and to say what other people want to hear—and therefore to learn how to stand up for ourselves.

4

"Whoever makes good progress in the beginning has all the more difficulties later on."

- Kyudo Zen Master Awa Kenzô

Even for those who're convinced that meditation might be something worth doing, cultivating the discipline to sit in silence once per day and endure difficult emotions is challenging. The majority of people who start the practice don't stick with it long enough to see it work. What seem to be more pressing obligations or desires make meditation easy to skip. No one else notices when we miss the twenty-minute session we promised ourselves.

Even now, after years of practice, when I'm fully convinced of the importance of my meditation, I sometimes find myself willing to procrastinate when my list of things-to-do seems more urgent than sitting somewhere, silent and alone. But when I'm thinking clearly I understand that practicing meditation is one of the best ways I can spend the required time.

In both my junior and senior seasons, I finally realized that, for me, meditation was more important than getting 50 or 100 extra shots up. Whenever possible I did both, but no matter how much I practiced my shot, my mind had to be in order for the shot to work.

An initial inability to focus on the breath and quiet the mind discourages people. Those new to the practice often expect too much too soon, the same way a dieter hopes to lose 40 pounds in a month or two. Complicating the issue is the fact that these days meditation is commonly sold by authors and app developers as a cure-all for every variety of negative experiences. The difficulties faced in meditation are understated if not ignored by these people, and the benefits are exaggerated, especially for beginners. As a result, new meditation students tend to begin with the expectation of calm relaxation and a pleasant experience, and instead experience boredom, restlessness, and discomfort. Predictably common reactions are, "I'm not doing this right," or "Meditation isn't any good for me."

Here is Yongey Mingyur Rinpoche describing this problem:

"The first thing that happens when we begin to meditate, I told him, is that we learn just how crazy our minds are. Many of us take that as a sign that we are not cut out for meditation. Actually, it is just the opposite; it's the first sign you are becoming familiar with your own mind. It's a great insight. You will be fine."

If you decided that tomorrow you're going to start learning to play the violin, would you expect your first day, or even your first six months of practice, to turn you into a virtuoso? Even a much simpler skill, riding a bike, is frustrating at the start. But when you finally catch on you're able to hop onto the bike and, with little physical or mental effort, ride happily away. Meditation is no different—you have to push through the difficult beginning stages.

An additional confusion that disrupts consistent practice for beginners is that meditation is too often regarded as a metaphysical pill taken to calm the mind. Because the aim of meditation practice is ultimately to relax the mind and eliminate mental anguish, many aspiring meditators conclude that they should practice only when they're depressed or anxious, which is something like practicing high-jumping only after spraining an ankle.

I spent most of my first six months expecting meditation to calm me, and I became frustrated every time my mind wandered away from my object of focus: Why the hell can't I concentrate on my breath for more than three or four seconds at a time? I thought peaceful meditations were "good" and restless or sleepy meditations were "bad." I was wrong. In the Zen tradition, students are taught to appreciate the difficulties they face when they begin. In his book *Zen Mind, Beginner's Mind,* Shunryu Suzuki writes:

> "Those who can sit perfectly physically usually take more time to obtain the true way of Zen, the actual feeling of Zen, the marrow of Zen. But those who find great difficulties in practicing Zen will find more meaning in it."

The necessary shift occurred for me when I was told that what matters, especially in the beginning, is bringing attention back to the object of focus, over and over again. As various meditation teachers put it, bringing a wandering mind back to the object of attention is like a weightlifting repetition for the brain—each rep makes the mind slightly stronger, slightly more capable of dealing with distraction. So, when you begin to meditate, go easy on your expectations. Do your best to keep your attention focused, but, in the beginning, don't expect to be anywhere near perfect. Realize that moments when you catch your wandering mind and bring your attention back are victories, not failures.

CHAPTER 24

INSIGHTS

1

In 2018, Norway's 39 medals broke America's record for the most medals ever won in a winter Olympics. While it's logical to expect an Arctic country to produce great skaters and skiers, Norway also develops world class warm weather athletes, like Ada Hegerberg, one of the world's best female soccer players, and Anders Mol, possibly the world's best beach volleyball player. How can Norway, with a population of just over five million (the same as Minnesota), out-perform the historically athletic powerhouses of the U.S., Russia and China?

Journalist and researcher Tom Ferry has traveled the world studying how various countries and cultures develop athletes, and he claims that of all the systems he's seen, Norway's is the best, and that their strategy is simple: they try to make sure children love sports at an early age. Norway has a unique youth sports Bill of Rights that clearly defines a philosophy for athletic development.

For girls and boys from six to twelve years old, the focus is on making sports enjoyable. Gifted young athletes get no more attention than anyone else. The eventual result is that many of Norway's Olympic champions were in the middle of the pack at age ten. This is in stark contrast to the "tracking" that occurs in America, where, beginning at age six, the biggest and most talented athletes usually begin to receive better coaching and more attention than their smaller, less-gifted peers.

Tore Ovrebo, the head of Norway's Olympic training program, thinks that the Norwegian approach is not only healthier for children, but is the primary reason for the country's Olympic success. Though Norway's conduct likely seems soft and overly compassionate to many Americans, it consistently produces outstanding athletes. Ovrebo himself is highly competitive, and his goal is to dominate the rest of the world in the Olympic Games: "There is no collision between our ambition to be number one at the Olympic Winter Games and treating kids well. It's the same thing… When kids get emotionally prepared to have sport as their own project and ambition, then we start to rank them, and work with them in a totally different way… My main ambition here is to produce a high performance culture that can beat the rest of the world."

2

After Michael Jordan won his sixth championship, he was playing the piano and smoking a cigar while celebrating with his teammates. A reporter shouted at him, asking if he was coming back for another run at it. His response: "It's the moment! Stay in the moment! That's that Zen Buddhism shit, this is the moment."

Powerful incentives make young Americans want to succeed as athletes. Prominent among them is the hope of earning an athletic scholarship, which can save an athlete and her family tens (or hundreds) of thousands of dollars. The tiny percentage of athletes that go on from college to compete professionally in the major American sports earn extreme wealth. Beyond financial rewards, the social status that the best athletes enjoy is intoxicating for young minds to imagine. Girls and boys fantasize about becoming campus celebrities, scoring winning goals or touchdowns, and appearing on TV in front of millions of viewers. Parents have similar dreams about their sons and daughters.

The inevitable result is a hyper-competitive environment where promising young athletes and their families look toward future rewards at the expense of the present. As young, promising athletes grow up, the sense of play is often replaced by striving for status and aiming at future goals. Growing up, I was always tempted to view each season as a stepping stone to some later, greater end. The goal of a D-1 scholarship motivated me to train hard, but it also hovered over each game, practice, and season like a storm cloud. When I reflect on my athletic career, I realize that the joy and triumph I experienced when we won a district Little League championship was no less real or significant than winning a state championship in high school, or a big game in college. I wish that in my youth and adolescence I'd allowed myself to relax and enjoy my good fortune as an athlete, rather than fixating on vague future goals. When we focus too much on something other than the present, we diminish the value and beauty of sports.

3

If I'm blessed with children of my own, and they become athletes, I'll be careful not to put too much stress on them, physical or mental. I'll resist the pressures to ship my children to the most expensive and prestigious camps and showcases, and to the prominent AAU circuits. Many young, gifted athletes are burning out due to the extreme schedules they try to maintain. In recent years there's been a substantial increase in player injuries between ages 18 and 22. Dr. Marcus Elliott, the founder of P3 Applied Sports Science Lab, a training center specializing in athlete assessment, drew this conclusion when asked about modern youth basketball: "What they put their bodies through is so rigorous. It's so extreme. And a lot of them don't make it out to the other side." He goes so far as to call those who make it through without injury "survivors."

Kobe Bryant was a vocal critic of youth basketball and AAU culture throughout his career. He didn't think he could have lasted 20 years in the NBA if he'd taken on the modern youth schedule. He played one game every two weeks until he was 15 years old. Before that he shot and practiced ball handling every day, but not long enough for it to feel like work. Instead of playing in tournaments weekend after weekend, most of his work was on skill development and strength training.

Lebron James told Yahoo Sports that he regularly holds his children out of AAU games because he understands that their schedules are too demanding, jeopardizing young athletes' futures. I remember waking up on Sunday mornings after playing in four AAU games on a Saturday, feeling nearly crippled with stiffness and soreness.

In an interview about modern youth basketball, Wally Blase, a Chicago Bulls' athletic trainer from 1993-2000, revealed this about the man considered by many to be the greatest basketball player ever: "When the season ended,

Michael (Jordan) left and played golf and didn't pick up a basketball again until probably a little bit before training camp (in September)...He might have played pickup ball with some friends, but he wasn't working eight hours a day at some gym with some shooting coach."

Aside from the physical risks, a child who's overworked in adolescence will be at risk of mental burnout. I think sports can be a valuable activity for young people. And those who want to play in college need to make sacrifices. But finding some balance in life will set up a young athlete for a more sustainable and successful future.

4

Beyond mental training and improved life habits, a crucial variable in my recovery was the environment created by my Coaches Bergeson, Kaufman, Snyder, Long, and Tripp. Like teachers, coaches have the power to transform young people's lives.

The Netflix series *Last Chance U* documents the East LA Community College basketball team, which is made up of at risk young athletes who, through basketball, are given a chance to earn a degree and make something of themselves. I wonder how many people positively impact our society as much as coaches like John Mosely. I have the utmost respect and admiration for competent coaches who offer leadership and influence to young people who desperately need it.

Every day my teammates and I showed up at the gym and found determined, trustworthy coaches who knew the game well. I was motivated to give my best effort every day.

In poorly run athletic programs, turmoil between players and coaches is inevitable. Players who aren't motivated cut corners wherever and whenever they can. Unhappy players and coaches blame each other and feel mutually disconnected from a collective goal. In healthy programs, neither coaches nor players tolerate unproductive or irresponsible behavior because every individual feels a responsibility to the team. A large majority of programs fall somewhere between these extremes.

If I was going through the recruiting process again today, I'd be most concerned with finding a good coach and a good program, and I'd care much less about the level or perceived status of the school I chose.

Time spent in any noxious environment can lead to serious problems that reach beyond the court or the field: mental health issues, alcoholism, frustration that leads to dropping out of school. Many of us are youthfully overconfident, certain that we aren't influenced by those around us. But we all adapt to our environment to some extent, and it's easier to paddle with the current than against it.

5

Athletes should ask themselves these questions: "What am I especially good at?" "What does this team need that nobody else is contributing?" Those who can answer these questions will likely achieve increased success and find themselves enjoying their sport as a consequence. I should have known that my unique talent was spacing the floor and knocking down shots. Year after year, driving to the basket and trying to finish around the rim was diminishing my stock as a player.

My coaches told me after the season that I initially earned a spot in the rotation because of how hard I worked at practice every day, and because I consistently brought energy and toughness to the court. I played hard, even when I didn't feel like it. I fought through pain in drills and scrimmages, and I found time to get extra work outside of practice despite my heavy course load. Had I not done these things, I never would have been given the opportunity to find my shooting confidence in games.

On any team and in any given sport, a small percentage of players get most of the attention and praise. This is especially true in NBA basketball, where a few players command almost all the national attention. And this is what leads many young people to want to play like exceptionally skilled stars. But, for almost everybody, their efforts are counterproductive.

Former Oklahoma City Thunder forward Nick Collison's article, "How to Survive in the NBA When You're Not a Superstar," clarifies a rational strategy. He writes, "The goal is to try to make it very difficult for your team to replace you, so that they have to do what it takes to keep you around. That's how a player creates value for himself." In other words, understand what you can do on the court or the field, and do it very well. Certain skills—scoring, playmaking, home run hitting, closing out a baseball game in the bottom of the ninth, catching long touchdown passes—capture the attention of fans, while other actions crucial for a team's success never show up on a highlight reel. Collison again: "If you are a bench guy and you start to take more shots, to take your scoring average from six points a game up to eight points a game, not many people are going to notice. You are doing the same things, just in a more in-efficient way. On the other hand, if you average only five points a game but defensively you can blow up every pick and roll and take that option away from the opponent, you are going to be able to play for a long time and make a lot of money over your career."

Understanding what you can do that needs to be done, and doing it well, makes you valuable. Collison played 15 years in the NBA with Seattle/Oklahoma City, and in 2019 had his jersey retired at the arena. Over the course of his career he averaged 6 points and 5 rebounds in 20 minutes per game. More importantly, he brought exceptional toughness and energy to the court. His example applies to every level of team athletics.

<h1 style="text-align:center">6</h1>

When things got really hard, I desperately wanted to quit. If I did, I'd never have to see my coach again, or step into the gym I hated. I saw other students on campus who looked very happy to be living without pressure to perform. But I'm thankful that my family encouraged me to stick it out. Practically, I just couldn't justify giving up a scholarship and losing credits.

At the time I thought that basketball was causing my misery. Basketball was bad—we struggled as a team and we had a poor team culture. But I now realize that a lot of my problems were my own. It was like I was in a super messy room, with boxes piled up everywhere, cobwebs, old clothes and magazines scattered around, and mice running through the junk. The temptation is to pour gasoline everywhere, burn it all down and walk away. Just escape the problem and move on. As a player and a coach, and since then in my professional career, I've seen many people do this—when things get tough, they quit and walk away.

Sticking around means rummaging through the boxes, contending with all the mold and grime, and slowly and painfully sorting everything out—and sorting the situation out usually means you have to sort yourself out too.

Those who run from difficult times tend to continually find themselves in the same conditions again and again. The same dynamic applies to a job, in a creative project or a discipline, and it might be especially true in intimate relationships. When things get hard it's easy to imagine that a new and better partner will make things better. In sports it's a new coach or a new team that promises better days.

Sometimes it is wise to transfer from a team, leave a job or relationship, or give up on a project. But those who never stick around to work through their difficulties stay at the surface, and never resolve their issues with a team, a job, or a partner.

One of my friends quit the team after his sophomore season. He was a gifted player with prospects to play a lot and play well in the years to come. But he wanted to be just a student and enjoy his life. I envied him when he left. Midway through the following season he visited us and came to a house party near campus. He told me he wished he hadn't quit, and that he hoped to find another team the following year. I tried to console him by telling him, "Yeah, but don't forget how hard basketball is." He replied, "I remember, but life without basketball is fucking hard too."

7

The schedules that student athletes maintain often lead to envy of non-athletes on campus. I was jealous of students who could stay up all night doing homework without suffering any consequences the following day. Instead of writing a paper on a sunny afternoon, or going to the gym to get in some shooting between classes, they could either take a nap under a tree or throw a Frisbee on the quad. When I forced myself to bed at 10 o'clock Friday night I wondered what it might be like to go out to a party instead, with no practice scheduled for the morning. I envied the students who could go on backpacking trips and enjoy the beauty of Colorado while I was confined in a stuffy gym.

Sometimes my teammates and I felt this envy collectively. When we traveled by bus from one unremarkable town in South Dakota to another on a Friday night after a game, we'd scroll our social media apps and see our classmates at parties and music festivals, or skiing and snowboarding. Athletes with strong feelings for girls on campus often worry about leaving town for road games while the girls they like are out somewhere without them. This produced "The Red Shirt Spy Phenomenon," when traveling players ask the red shirts back home to go to the parties and report back if the girls they care about are dancing or hooking up with other guys. Traveling female athletes use the same tactic.

Some athletes do their best to function in many worlds—as a team member, a committed student, a member of the drugs and party culture, an expert video gamer, and so on. But responsible team members can't realistically find their pleasures in the relative freedom that non-athletes enjoy. Sacrifice is a large part of what makes the athletic experience unique. Shared struggles lead to deep bonds and friendships. And athletes tend to forget that non-athletes who attend sporting events look at those who compete with envy, wondering what it would be like to wear the uniform and go to battle in front of a crowd. The grass doesn't always look greener, but it often does.

8

It's important to understand the difference between self-discipline and self-suppression. Self-suppression is the act of concealing your true nature and what you really want to do in life in order to "get along." Self-discipline is letting your highest desires rule over lower desires—keeping the central core of your purpose firmly in mind and sacrificing short term desires for its benefit. Athletics, especially in college, are so demanding that it makes little sense to try to fulfill your commitment unless it's what you really want to do.

During my senior year my purpose was basketball, meditation, academics, and my relationships with my best friend and my new girlfriend. As I sacrificed nearly everything else for those commitments, I felt a sense of relief. Doing less actually led to more enjoyment and fulfillment.

9

"Heroes are heroes because they are heroic in behavior, not because they won or lost."

- Nassim Taleb

After failing to lead the Cavaliers to a championship, Lebron James joined Dwayne Wade and Chris Bosh on the Miami Heat and made the NBA finals in their first season together. Lebron had a dismal series, scoring only 8 points in a crucial game 4 loss. Miami eventually lost in 6 games to the underdog Mavericks.

In the following season, he found himself on the brink of another failure, down 3-2 to the Boston Celtics before Game 6 on the road. In many of his previous playoff failings he'd played cowardly, often looking weirdly detached, and seemed to quit in moments of deep adversity. But in this game, despite his fears and insecurities about his playoff reputation, he faced the game with bravery and resolve. He played with a stone-cold, stoic demeanor and determination that neither his fans nor detractors had seen before, scored 45 points, led his team to victory, and ultimately won his first NBA title. In fact, even if he'd lost that game, or lost the series, the way he played was unarguably courageous. The fear he felt, and the way he showed up despite the fear, made it courageous.

I think many modern people have become confused about what it actually means to be courageous. For most of my playing career I thought being afraid was a bad thing. I thought courage was the absence of fear, and that I was courageous only when I felt confident and relaxed. But I was mistaken. If Lebron James showed up somewhere to play high school basketball next year, his performance would be dominant, but not courageous.

As a senior, I finally understood this. Before games I felt afraid of failing, anxious that I'd lose my spot in the starting lineup, or let my teammates and coaches down. I finally recognized that my fear wasn't a shortcoming, but rather something that gave me an opportunity to show courage. I became able to play freely and passionately despite my fears. My mental training helped me become more comfortable with not knowing what was going to happen next. What I learned was that I didn't have to have control over the outcome in order to be okay.

Athletes (and everyone else) should understand that the goal isn't to get rid of anxiety or fear, but to deal with it skillfully. Athletes who feel no nervousness before a big game are probably not in the right mindset for competition. Playing sports, or doing anything that involves taking risks, comes with uncomfortable feelings of uncertainty. If we never felt this, we'd never truly feel alive. It's the uncertainty, and the chance for success or failure that make sports so captivating.

Without fear, anxiety, insecurity, or self doubt, there would be no opportunity to be courageous.

10

"Every virtue carried to an extreme, degenerates into folly or positive vice."

- an applicable quote misattributed to Aristotle

What does it mean to be a good teammate and buy into the program? It's not as simple as always sacrificing yourself for the collective, and always maintaining goodwill with teammates. It's good to get along with teammates, but not to such a degree that you sacrifice your presence on the court. Good coaches love players who sacrifice for the collective, but not players who kiss their asses and try to gain favor by barking out exactly what they want to hear. The best players maintain some individuality, and rather than repressing their darker impulses so they can get along, they channel them into something productive.

Many athletes find themselves relating to their teammates by outwardly keeping the peace and backing down from any conflict, while they internally wish failure upon their friends. These athletes can trick themselves into thinking that their lack of friction between teammates and coaches is somehow virtuous, even though their inward intentions are unhealthy.

Part of my development as both a player and a person was learning to stand up for myself: to fight for more playing time and greater status within the team, to take no shit from teammates and opponents, and to say what I thought. And, at the same time, I truly wanted my teammates and friends to be happy on the inside, even the friends I sometimes fought with at practice. I wasn't perfect at this, and I'm still not, but that's the direction I'm trying to move in.

For people pleasers who like to keep the peace, this is an indispensable form of development.

11

If I could start my college athletic career over, I'd diversify my identity, understanding that interests and pursuits outside of sports can actually enhance your athletic career. I'd be more rational about my relationship with drugs and partying. I'd sometimes go out and drink with my friends, but I wouldn't abuse alcohol weekend after weekend. I'd smoke pot only on occasion, and only if I wasn't subject to random tests. I wouldn't rely on alcohol or pot to fall asleep, and I'd learn to approach girls without getting drunk first. I'd abstain from cigarettes, cocaine, and Adderall. I'd spend much less time on my phone, and during study times I'd keep my phone off and out of sight.

I'd focus on sustainability and mental clarity, understanding that real improvements come from making many small, correct decisions over and over again. I'd focus on my habits instead of on goals, and I'd simplify my life and be okay missing out on things that my friends were doing.

Each offseason I'd take an extended break from my sport and try to do something out of my comfort zone— backpacking, traveling to a different culture, or attending a meditation retreat. I understand that a yearly mental and physical reset is essential. Upon return I'd train hard for the upcoming season and make sure I showed up to campus in great shape.

I'd be consistent and focused in my training, and I'd favor shorter, crisper, more intense bursts than drawn out workouts. I'd focus on the basics of the game before attempting to develop flashy or complex skills. I'd be mindful during training, focusing on how my mind felt during my reps in the weight room and on the court. I'd practice non-judgmental awareness and concentration, rather than self-criticism and frustration.

In competition I'd understand that success requires taking risks and making myself vulnerable to failure. I'd try to stand up to my fears, understanding that shrinking from them only exaggerates them. I'd compete hard every day, I wouldn't shy away from conflict, and I'd bring serious energy to the court.

I'd wish my teammates well and enjoy my time with them, realizing that jealousies and friction with my friends and teammates over girls, playing time, or success will eventually be seen as wastes of time and energy.

And I'd protect my sleep and always make time for my daily, formal meditation practice.

12

The World War II novel *From Here to Eternity* was written by James Jones, who fought in the war, served time in an army stockade, and adapted his own experiences as he created his characters. Two major characters, Prewitt and Maggio, find themselves together in the Schofield Barracks stockade in Hawaii, and each is punished with several days of solitary confinement in a dark, cramped, miserable place known as "the hole." These tough, rugged soldiers somehow discovered that the only way to stay sane and reduce suffering while doing time in the hole was to focus on their breathing. Following and counting their breaths kept prisoners' minds from degenerating into fear and dread. Fictional evidence like this, based on real experience and portrayed believably, does as much as reading about a new brain scan to convince me that meditation works.

I encourage athletes and coaches to give the practice of meditation a serious try, and then decide whether or not it's helpful. I don't encourage athletes who connect with the practice to view it as a panacea that will solve all of life's problems, or to use the practice as a way to retreat from sports and life. But I know that meditation can become an integral part of both a successful playing career and a good life.

13

Like many young athletes, I'd misunderstood why competition matters, because I became addicted to the buzz of winning at an early age. Whether it was math competitions in class, kickball on the playground, or monopoly with my family, I wanted to win. I was so competitive growing up that family members often told me to loosen up—but I feared that if I loosened up I'd stop winning. At higher levels of basketball my hyper-competitive attitude did more harm than good. Here's what Tim Gallwey writes in *The Inner Game of Tennis*:

> "It is when competition is thus used as a means of creating a self-image relative to others that the worst in a person tends to come out; then the ordinary fears and frustrations become greatly exaggerated. If I am secretly afraid that playing badly or losing the match may be taken to mean that I am less of a man, naturally I am going to be more upset with myself for missing shots. And, of course, this very uptightness will make it more difficult for me to perform at my highest levels. There would be no problem with competition if one's self-image were not at stake."

Later, when I struggled in basketball and finally discovered meditation practice and eastern philosophy, I swung in the opposite direction, and again misunderstood competition.

I decided that competition was at odds with living well. In hindsight I realize that my reaction was a defense mechanism meant to make what I was failing at unimportant. Gallwey again:

> "But whereas some seem to get trapped in the compulsion to succeed, others take a rebellious stance. Pointing to the blatant cruelties and limitations involved in a cultural pattern which tends to value only the winner and ignore even the positive qualities of the mediocre, they vehemently criticize competition. Among the most vocal are youth who have suffered under competitive pressures imposed on them by parents or society. Teaching these young people, I often observe in them a desire to fail. They seem to seek failure by making no effort to win or achieve success. They go on strike, as it were."

As a college senior I loved competition again, but with a new attitude that I at first had trouble understanding. I couldn't find the balance between cooperation and competition. Was competition really at odds with loving and connecting to others? Gallwey writes that he struggled with this paradox for much of his life before finally coming to understand that competition itself isn't the problem, but the way we tend to relate to it is.

> "Once one recognizes the value of having difficult obstacles to overcome, it is a simple matter to see the true benefit that can be gained from competitive sports. In tennis who is it that provides a person with the obstacles he needs in order to experience

his highest limits? His opponent, of course! Then is your opponent a friend or an enemy? He is a friend to the extent that he does his best to make things difficult for you. Only by playing the role of your enemy does he become your true friend. Only by competing with you does he in fact cooperate! In this use of competition it is the duty of your opponent to create the greatest possible difficulties for you, just as it is yours to try to create obstacles for him. Only by doing this do you give each other the opportunity to find out to what heights each can rise."

It wasn't until the last game of my college career that I truly understood this. The gratitude I felt for the opposing team, and for all of my struggles as a player, stemmed from this realization. Alan Watts echoed this sentiment, pointing out that what looks like brutal competition at one level, is actually cooperation at another. The various kinds of cells in our bodies are in a brutal competition, without which we wouldn't survive. The animals and plants in the food chain engage in brutal competition, and this preserves the balance of the natural world.

One of the beauties of sports is to teach young people to relate to competition in a healthy and honorable way. Understanding this can transform the way you view your sport. You can discover that the ultimate goal isn't to stack trophies in a case and see your name in record books, but rather to find levels of excellence and grace that wouldn't be possible without the obstacles and adversities that sports provide.

When you accept this view, when the opponent's best player is injured and has to leave a big game, there will be part of you that's disappointed. Even though you'll now have an easier path to victory, you've been robbed of an opportunity to push yourself to new limits. You'll understand that respecting your opponent enables you to give full effort to the game. Gallwey again:

"Today I play every point to win. It's simple and it's good. I don't worry about winning or losing the match, but whether or not I am making the maximum effort during every point because I realize that that is where the true value lies."

CHAPTER 25

LIFE AFTER SPORTS

1

"The athlete dies twice."

- Steve Nash

Swimmer Michael Phelps won 28 Olympic medals, 23 of them gold, and had this to say on the subject of life after the Olympics: "We're lost... because we spent four years grinding for that one moment. And now, we don't know what the hell to do. I think it's safe to say that a good 80%—maybe more—go through some kind of post Olympic depression." Phelps said he contemplated suicide after his second arrest for driving under the influence.

Most athletes end their careers at age 18, or 22, or, for a very few, between 25 and 40. And many of them, because they're young, have given little thought to the fact that they'll have to dedicate themselves to something else for their remaining years. Obviously, many former athletes find it difficult to adjust to life in the world at large. Paradoxically, it's often those who have enjoyed the most athletic success—like Phelps—who find life after sports most challenging. Athletes who have seen their names in headlines and heard crowds screaming for them are soon forgotten once their careers end. Names die, and men and women remain.

Playing sports is, in many ways, excellent preparation for the world at large. Among other things, athletes learn how to push out of their comfort zones for the sake of necessary growth, and how to be accountable to others. They learn that things don't always go your way even when you do your very best, and how to respond to pressure and criticism. Student athletes learn how to manage a busy schedule and prioritize tasks.

But in other ways, a committed student athlete can be handicapped when a career ends. Sports are clean and well organized, as close as anything we know to a true meritocracy. There are agreed upon rules and regulations, and the objective, to put the ball in the basket, or kick the ball into the net, and to prevent your opponents from doing so, is always perfectly clear. This structure is reinforced in academics—to get an A you have to follow the professor's instructions and complete the required tasks successfully and on time.

Life outside sports and school often becomes messy and complicated. With fewer rules, it's often less fair. There are no painted lines surrounding you, and no coaches or professors guiding your behavior, which is why student athletes who've grown accustomed to structure and clear objectives can struggle with the freedom and messiness of life in a much enlarged world.

When my career ended I had no coach to report to, or season to prepare for, or assignments to complete. Instead, there was a jarring lack of direction and too much free time to fill. I hadn't been free from a season to prepare for in over a decade, and now I had to create a new life. I knew how to work hard, but didn't know what to work on.

Every year, hundreds of thousands of us face this reality, and with no obligation to be ready to perform, it's easy to abandon the beneficial habits that can keep athletes happy—adequate sleep, physical exercise, a healthy diet, and consistent meditation. To make things worse, athletes who customarily worked off elevated numbers of calories every day experience drastically reduced metabolic rates, and eat as much or more than ever.

Lingering nostalgically on the glory days isn't a useful pastime, much less a way of life. Ex-athletes have to make serious efforts to find worthwhile pursuits. Consider Kobe Bryant reflecting on his retirement: "Fast-forward 20 years from now: If basketball is the best thing I've done in my life, then I've failed. It's a very simple mission, very simple quest, very simple goal. These next 20 years need to be better than the previous 20." Before Bryant's life tragically ended, he was living his commitment, and engaged in bold pursuits that transcended sports and basketball. He remains a model for us all.

2

"Humans don't mind hardship, in fact they thrive on it; what they mind is not feeling necessary. Modern society has perfected the art of making people not feel necessary."
- Sebastian Junger, *Tribe*

For me, and for many other former athletes that I've spoken to, the most challenging aspect of transitioning out of sports is losing the social connections that come from being on a team. I took for granted this aspect of sports throughout my entire life. Every new season the world handed me a batch of best friends and a sense of purpose as we tried to create the best season we could manage, both individually and collectively. Who would have thought that the parts of sports I hated, like waking up at 5 am to lift weights, or showing up ready to compete even when I felt sad or lethargic, and sharing this struggle with my best friends, was secretly giving my life meaning and fulfillment?

I enjoy having the freedom to pursue things outside of sports, but I'm still learning how to find social connections that resemble those from the locker room. The sterile, benign jokes at the corporate water cooler are not nearly as joyful as the outlandish locker room banter I'd taken for granted.

Now that I've graduated, and many of my best friends have moved to different cities, and there's no structure in my life that connects me to friends on a daily basis, I've discovered how hard it is to create real bonds and friendships. I never had to learn how to make friends, because I had friends in every locker room and every bus trip throughout my entire life. I wrote above about how painful it is to not contribute to your tribe, but not having a tribe is another form of deep pain.

Exercise, meditation, productivity, creativity, financial success, clean eating, cold showers; all of these are great things to do and pursue, but you probably won't be healthy or happy if you're lonely and isolated as you do them, which tends to happen to many athletes when they leave their sport. In recent years I've become more deliberate in putting things on the calendar with my old athletic friends. If you don't set dates and purchase plane tickets, years can pass without seeing your best friends.

I also find deep meaning and fulfillment in my committed relationship with Rebecca, and the most wise people in my life tell me that starting a family offers the sense of purpose and connection that many of us are missing.

I recommend that athletes who finish their careers take this problem seriously, and make deep, lasting relationships a priority. Modern society can be extremely isolating. Without the locker room, you have to find ways to make it happen yourself.

3

"The development of inner skills is required, but it is interesting to note that if, while learning tennis, you begin to learn how to focus your attention and how to trust in yourself, you have learned something far more valuable than how to hit a forceful backhand. The backhand can be used to advantage only on a tennis court, but the skill of mastering the art of effortless concentration is invaluable in whatever you set your mind to."

- Tim Gallwey, *The Inner Game of Tennis*

My career ended just as I began to understand what it means to truly connect with teammates and coaches, to become immersed in the flow of the game and play with pure passion and joy. When I watch tapes of players like Tim Duncan and Ichiro, I see athletes who reached levels of mental excellence that I never came close to.

My hope is that sharing my experiences will encourage young athletes to train their own minds and experience the precious benefits.

It's never too soon to begin. My mom teaches gentle mindfulness to her second graders. When I sat in on her class I was surprised to see how quickly children understood and learned the practice. Instead of regarding meditation as just another chore, as adults often do, second graders were excited about it, begging her to have them sit quietly, and happy to talk about how they used their mindful practice throughout their days. Children's brains enjoy peak neuroplasticity, enabling them to learn languages, music, sports, and undoubtedly mindfulness, far more quickly than adults. Spending a year in Germany when she was five years old, and enrolled in a German kindergarten, Mom spoke German fluently in a matter of months. Now as an adult, she sees her students learning to handle their "big emotions" in a positive way.

Because sports offer a healthy level of adversity, mental training in the context of sports is an obvious way to prepare young people for adversities certain to face them in life itself. So, with mental training incorporated into youth sports, we'll see more happy athletes who become happy and productive adults.

When I play recreational basketball now I'm still an accurate shooter, and I have fun. I don't regret the countless hours I spent practicing shooting and ball handling, but I'm often struck by the fact that I'm still good at something with very little utility in my life. In contrast to that, the hours I spent as an athlete sitting in silent meditation, training my attention to be more reliably focused on what matters, continue to deliver valuable returns that apply to everything I do. Mental training benefits my relationships, my productivity, and my general sense of well-being. I love the discipline of daily meditation.

I initially adopted meditation with the hopes that it could calm my anxiety, improve my play, and allow me to enjoy sports again. Since graduating, I've explored more advanced methods of meditation and gone on several silent retreats, meditating for 12 hours per day without speaking, reading, writing, or exercising. These experiences have produced some of the most interesting and enjoyable moments of my life, and I've come to understand that the power of meditation can be far more than a tool for greater concentration and performance—it's a way to truly connect with the present moment, which is all we ever have. The mental training that prepared me for the adversity of sport also prepared me for the adversities of life itself—adversities that make a bad stretch of games or an injury seem trivial in comparison. When a loved one is sick and dying, will your mind spin out of control, or will you face the situation with grace?

While mental training is, in some sense, preparation for the worst times of our lives, it also prepares us to genuinely connect with the precious moments that make life well worth living. In a culture that continues to value increased speed, and novelty of experience, sitting still once a day serves as a necessary anchor—an opportunity to drop everything and deliberately pay attention to the present moment, to appreciate the beauty and mystery of existence. Just as an athletic career is short and precious, so is life. Shouldn't we cultivate minds that make the most of it?

To find resources for meditation in the context of athletics visit Billyhansen.net, or scan the QR code below.

ACKNOWLEDGMENTS

First, to my Opa, Michael Baughman, who met me every day after school to rebound while I practiced my jumpshot, and spent time for years reading my work and teaching me to write clearly. Opa introduced me to the joy and power of reading and writing, and his love and wisdom have largely shaped who I've become. Without his help and guidance this book would not have been written.

To my Dad, who helped me fall in love with sports. I had to grow up before I understood that not all dads ice their arm every summer night and attend physical therapy appointments so they can keep throwing batting practice, and neither do they stand outside stadiums and arenas after professional games to befriend security guards so their children can meet their athletic heroes. After each game I played I knew I'd have a long text waiting for me, either celebrating my success or encouraging me after failure. Part of the joy of my final season was knowing how intently Dad watched each game, and how happy it made him to see me do well.

To my Mom and Oma, whose unconditional love and support anchor my life. I have a wonderful mother, and I can't possibly explain here how much she's meant to me. Through my struggles as a college athlete, it was often my phone calls with Mom and Oma that kept me going, and college visits home to spend time at Mom's and Oma's houses offered peace and joy.

To Alan Hess, who held my hand through the confusing and overwhelming publishing process, and saved me from making some serious mistakes.

To Coach Porter and Coach Daniels, for giving me the opportunity to play college basketball, and for treating me with love and respect despite my struggles. To Steve Ledesma, whose care and support helped me through my darkest days as a player.

To Dylan King, Rio Pedersen, Bryan Siefker, and Jarrett Green. Their warmth and friendship were the reasons I stuck it out and didn't quit.

To Dr. Taylor, Dr. Grassi and Dr. Seibert, the inspiring professors who went out of their way to help me find an academic direction and support me throughout my time at Regis.

To Jeni Shannon, the wise and gentle counselor who introduced me to meditation, and thereby changed my life.

To Libby Edson, whose friendship and support assisted me enormously in my time as a player and throughout this project.

To Don Senestrero, who helped me develop as a player and a man, and who serves as a model for anyone who wants to live life fully.

To Brady Bergeson, who saved my love for sports, and inspired me to live sincerely and with passion.

To the many other coaches who helped shape me as an athlete and as a man: Michael Humphrey, Steve Dodds, Darrell Hegdahl, Jeff Schlecht, Abdi Guled, Scott Mickey, Josh Leedy, Paul Westthelle, Jeff Turner, Charlie Hall, Clint Bryan, Nathe Sutor, Larry Kellems, Tony Akpan, Nate Maybin, Sandee Kensinger, Benjamin Kaufman, Dan Snyder, Kyle Long, and Kenny Tripp.

To the teammates and friends who made me laugh and shared the ups and downs of competitive sports with me.

And finally, to Rebecca, who makes me truly happy, and has loved and supported me through the highs and the lows.

ABOUT THE AUTHOR

Billy Hansen played basketball at Regis University in Denver and served as an assistant coach there for two years after his playing career ended. He presently teaches a course at Regis called Mindfulness for Athletes, and is the meditation coach for the Regis men's basketball and baseball teams. His specialty is "mindful shooting"—training basketball players in the mental side of shooting the ball—and he's worked with athletes at all levels, from high school to the NBA. With a bachelor's degree in mathematics and a master's in data science, he's also a data scientist and writer.

'on can be obtained
com